OFFICE XP

in easy steps

STEPHEN COPESTAKE

COMPUTER STEP

In easy steps is an imprint of Computer Step
Southfield Road . Southam
Warwickshire CV47 0FB . England

http://www.ineasysteps.com

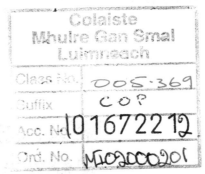
Notice of Liability

Every effort has been made to ensure that this book contains accurate
and current information. However, Computer Step and the author shall
not be liable for any loss or damage suffered by readers as a result of
any information contained herein.

Trademarks

Microsoft®, Windows® and Office XP® are registered trademarks of
Microsoft Corporation. All other trademarks are acknowledged as
belonging to their respective companies.

Printed and bound in the United Kingdom

ISBN 1-84078-137-8

Table of Contents

Using speech recognition

4

A common approach

This chapter shows you how to get started quickly in any Office XP module. You'll create new documents and open/save existing ones. You'll use the Shortcut bar to save time and energy, and also get information you need from on-line HELP and Ask-a-Question. Finally, you'll edit files from Internet Explorer and enhance your use of Office with additional features (these include Quick File Switching, error repair, copying/pasting multiple items, using the Task Pane, signing documents digitally and document imaging).

Covers

Chapter One

Introduction

The standard edition of Microsoft Office XP consists of four modules:

*   Word 2002 – word-processor

*   Excel 2002 – spreadsheet

*   PowerPoint 2002 – presentation/slide show creator

*   Outlook 2002 – personal/business information manager

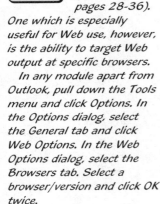

There are many new features in Office XP (in particular, see pages 28-36). One which is especially useful for Web use, however, is the ability to target Web output at specific browsers.

In any module apart from Outlook, pull down the Tools menu and click Options. In the Options dialog, select the General tab and click Web Options. In the Web Options dialog, select the Browsers tab. Select a browser/version and click OK twice.

Three at least of these programs are leaders in their respective fields. The point about Office, however, is that it integrates the four modules exceptionally well. With the exception of Outlook, which has to adopt a relatively individualistic approach, the modules share a common look and feel.

The illustration below shows the Word opening screen. Flagged are components which are common to PowerPoint, Outlook and Excel, too. (There are also, of course, differences between the module screens: Outlook, for instance, because of its very different nature, has fewer toolbars. We'll explore this in later chapters.)

Title bar   Menu bar   Toolbar

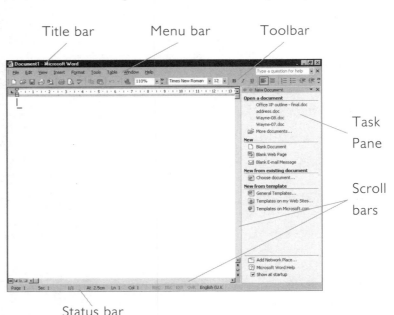

Task Pane

Scroll bars

Status bar

Toolbars

To add a new button to a toolbar, right-click over the toolbar. Click Customize. In the dialog which launches, click the Commands tab. In the Categories field, click a category (a group of associated icons). In the Commands box, drag a button onto the toolbar in the open document. Finally, click Close.

Toolbars are important components in all four Office XP modules. A toolbar is an on-screen bar which contains shortcut buttons. These symbolise and allow easy access to often-used commands which would normally have to be invoked via one or more menus.

For example, Word 2002's Standard toolbar lets you:

- create, open, save and print documents
- perform copy & paste and cut & paste operations
- undo editing actions
- insert a hyperlink

by simply clicking on the relevant button.

Toolbars vary to some extent from module to module. We'll be looking at these in more detail as we encounter them. For the moment, some general advice:

Specifying which toolbars are displayed

In any Office module, pull down the View menu and click Toolbars. Now do the following:

This is Word's toolbar list. Available toolbars in the other Office XP programs vary slightly.

The Task Pane is a toolbar. To hide or show it, untick or tick the Task Pane entry.
   (For more information on using the Task Pane, see page 33).

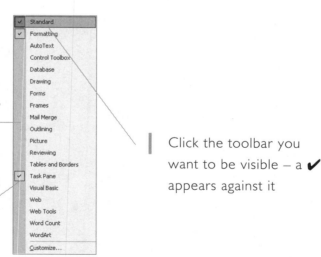

Click the toolbar you want to be visible – a ✔ appears against it

Repeat this procedure for as many toolbars as necessary.

Automatic customisation

As you use the Office XP modules, individual features are dynamically promoted or demoted in the relevant menus.
   This means menus are continually evolving...

Until Office 2000, it was true that, although different users use different features, no allowance had been made for this: the same features displayed on everyone's menus and toolbars...

Now, however, menus and toolbars are personalised in Office XP modules.

Personalised menus

When you first use a module, its menus display the features which Microsoft believes are used 95% of the time. Features which are infrequently used are not immediately visible. This is made clear in the illustrations below:

Office XP menus expand automatically. Simply pull down the required menu, (which will at first be abbreviated) then wait a few seconds: it expands to display the full menu.
   However, to expand them manually, click here on the chevrons at the bottom of the menu:

Word 2002's Format menu, as it first appears...

Automatic customisation also applies to toolbars. Note the following:

• *if possible, they display on a single row*

• *they overlap when there isn't enough room on-screen*

• *icons are 'promoted' and 'demoted' like menu entries*

• *demoted icons are shown in a separate fly-out, reached by clicking:*

...the expanded menu

Creating new documents

With the exception of Outlook (see Chapter 6), all Office XP modules let you:

*   create new blank documents

*   create new documents based on a 'template'

*   create new documents with the help of a 'Wizard'

Because Word 2002, PowerPoint 2002 and Excel 2002 are uniform in the way they create new documents, we'll look at this topic here rather than in the later chapters, which are specific to each program.
(However, see Chapter 5 for specialised advice on creating new slide shows.)

Creating blank documents is the simplest route to new document creation; use this if you want to define the document components yourself from scratch. This is often not the most efficient or effective way to create new documents.

Templates – also known as boilerplates – are sample documents complete with the relevant formatting and/or text. By basing a new document on a template, you automatically have access to these.

Wizards are advanced templates which incorporate a question-and-answer system. You work through a series of dialogs, answering the appropriate questions and making the relevant choices.

Documents created with the use of templates or Wizards can easily be amended subsequently.

The topics that relate to templates and Wizards do not apply to Outlook.

Both templates and Wizards are high-powered yet easy to use shortcuts to document creation. Office XP provides a large number of templates and Wizards.

Launching the New dialog

Utilise any of the following methods:

A.   Using the Start menu

When Office is installed, it amends the Windows Start menu. Carry out the following procedure:

The New dialog is crucial to creating new documents based on templates and wizards.

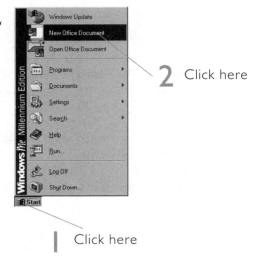

2   Click here

Click here

B.   From within the program

In Word 2002, Excel 2002 or PowerPoint 2002, refer to the Task Pane on the right of the screen and do the following:

To create a new blank document in Word, PowerPoint and Excel, press Ctrl+N.

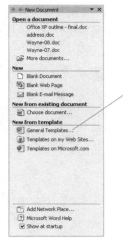

Click General Templates
(but see page 14 for how to
use Web-based templates)

Using the New dialog

To use the module-specific New dialog, follow method B on the facing page. Now carry out steps 1-3 on the right.

The form the New dialog takes depends, to some extent, on which method you use to launch it. If you invoke it by using the Start button, you get the full version which incorporates elements from Word, Excel and PowerPoint. You can then choose which type of new document you want to create.

If, on the other hand, you call up the New dialog from within Word, Excel or PowerPoint, you get an abbreviated form specific to the program.

If you base a new document on a template, Office creates a detailed document with preset (editable) text and formatting. If you use a wizard, on the other hand, you get a succession of dialogs:

Using the full New dialog

First launch the New dialog (see step A on the facing page). Then do the following:

Activate the relevant tab

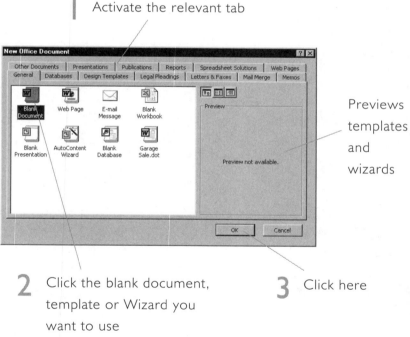

Previews templates and wizards

Complete these as appropriate. The end result is the same as using a template: a feature-rich document you can edit as necessary.

2 Click the blank document, template or Wizard you want to use

3 Click here

After step 3, further dialogs may launch if you're using a template or wizard — complete these by following the on-screen instructions.

In the above illustration, a new blank Word document is being created.

Opening Office XP documents

For how to open existing contacts or tasks in Outlook 2002, see Chapter 6.

We saw earlier that Office XP lets you create new documents in various ways. You can also open Word 2002, Excel 2002 and PowerPoint 2002 documents you've already created.

In any module apart from Outlook, refer to the Task Pane on the right of the screen and perform steps 1-2 (if you haven't recently opened the document you want to open, carry out steps 3-4 instead):

In Excel 2002, (providing you're using Internet Explorer 4.01 or higher) you can interact with Web-based spread-sheets you open using the procedures on the facing page. For instance, you can:

- *enter data*
- *create formulas*
- *recalculate and sort/filter data*
- *perform basic formatting*

directly from within the browser.

You can open documents based on Web templates. In step 3, click Templates on Microsoft.com instead. Now follow the on-screen instructions.

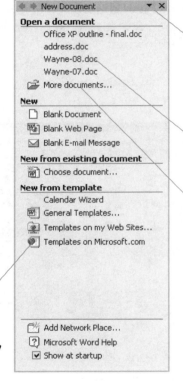

1 If your Task Pane doesn't look like this, click the arrow and select New Document, New Workbook or New Presentation in the menu

2 Click an existing document to open it

3 If the document you want to open isn't listed, click More Documents

You can also launch the Open dialog directly from within any module except Outlook. Press Ctrl+O.

4 Use the Open dialog to find and select the file you want to open. Click Open

Opening Internet/Intranet documents

In any of the Office modules (apart from Outlook), you can open documents stored at FTP sites on the World Wide Web or on Intranets.

If the Web toolbar isn't currently on-screen, move the mouse pointer over any existing toolbar and right-click. In the menu which appears, click Web. Now do the following:

To open Internet documents, you must have a live connection to the Internet.

After step 4, the Web/ Intranet site selected in step 3 is opened in your browser.

Click Go

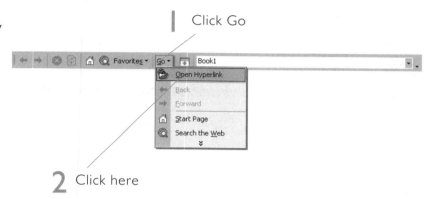

2 Click here

3 Type in the relevant address

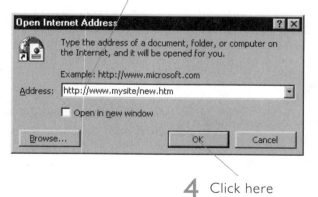

4 Click here

Saving Office XP documents

It's important to save your work at frequent intervals, in order to avoid data loss in the event of a hardware fault or power interruption. With the exception of Outlook, Office XP uses a consistent approach to saving.

Saving a document for the first time

In Word, Excel or PowerPoint, pull down the File menu and click Save. Or press Ctrl+S. Now do the following:

Re step 2 – click any buttons here: for access to the relevant folders.

(For instance, to save files to your Desktop, click Desktop.)

2 Click here. In the drop-down list, click a drive/ folder combination

Note that you can use a shortcut for either save method.
In Word, Excel or PowerPoint, click this icon:

in the Standard toolbar.

3 Type in a file name

4 Click here

Click here. In the list, click the format you want to save to

Saving previously saved documents

In Word, Excel or PowerPoint, pull down the File menu and click Save. Or press Ctrl+S. No dialog launches; instead, Office XP saves the latest version of your document to disk, overwriting the previous version.

In Word 2002, you can use a special wizard to create Web pages. In the Task Pane, click General Templates. In the New dialog, select the Web Pages tab. Double-click Web Page Wizard and follow the on-screen instructions.

Saving to the Internet

In any of the Office XP modules (apart from Outlook), you can save documents (usually in HTML – HyperText Markup Language – format) to network, Web or FTP servers. You can do this so long as you've created a shortcut to the folder that contains them.

Creating shortcuts to Web/FTP folders

Open the Word, Excel or PowerPoint Open or Save As dialog and do the following:

3 Double-click Add Network Place

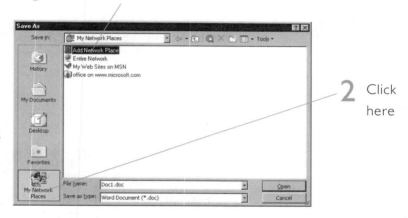

2 Click here

4 Complete the Add Network Place wizard

Saving to shortcuts

Pull down the File menu and click Save As Web Page. In Word, click in the Save as type: field and select Web Page or Web Page, Filtered (the final option strips out most Word-specific formatting and produces much smaller file sizes); in Excel or PowerPoint, select Web Page. Complete the rest of the dialog in the normal way then select a destination shortcut and a destination format. Click OK.

Editing in Internet Explorer

Using the technique discussed here, Office XP files, converted to HTML format and saved to the Web can be run by the majority of Internet users.

When you create HTML files from within Office XP modules (see below), they can be edited from within Internet Explorer 5.X/6.

Look at the illustration below:

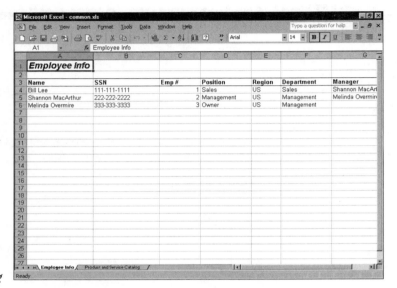

See chapter 5 for how to run slide shows in Internet Explorer itself.

After step 1, the file is opened within the originating Office XP module, with the formatting intact despite the 'round-trip'.

Use standard editing techniques to make the relevant amendments.

This is a simple Excel 2002 worksheet. You can use the techniques discussed on page 17 to convert it to a HTML file – see 'Saving to shortcuts'. Once the HTML file has been opened in Internet Explorer, do the following:

Click the toolbar Edit icon (its precise form reflects the original Office module):

You may not be able to accurately edit HTML files in Internet Explorer if they were created in Word with the Filtered HTML export option – see page 17.

Saving configuration settings

You can use a special wizard – the Save My Settings Wizard – to save configuration details in a special file (with the extension .ops). You can then restore the details in the file as a way of transferring your Office XP settings to another machine, or as a backup for your existing PC.

Using the Save My Settings Wizard

You could save configuration details on your Web site, as a handy backup.

1 Close all Office programs

2 Click Start, Programs, Microsoft Office Tools, Save My Settings Wizard

Not closing all modules can result in faulty configuration details being written.

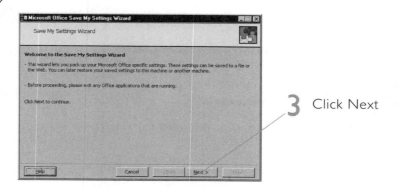

3 Click Next

4 Click Save... to save configuration details, or Restore... to implement previously saved settings

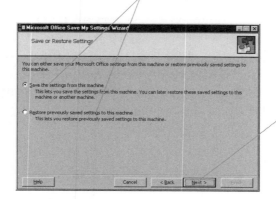

5 Click Next and complete the subsequent dialogs

Using Office's HELP system

Office calls these highly specific HELP bubbles 'ToolTips'.

ToolTips are a specialised form of ScreenTips (see below).

Office supports the standard Windows HELP system. For instance:

*   Moving the mouse pointer over toolbar buttons produces an explanatory HELP bubble:

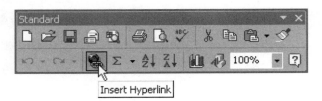

*   You can move the mouse pointer over fields in dialogs, commands or screen areas and produce a specific HELP box. Carry out the following procedure to achieve this:

Office calls these highly specific HELP topics 'ScreenTips'.

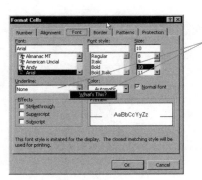

Right-clicking a field and left-clicking the box which launches...

Select an underline type to format the selected text with an underline.

...produces a specific HELP topic

Other standard Windows HELP features are also present; see your Windows documentation for how to use these. Additionally, all the Office XP applications have inbuilt HELP in the normal way...

Ask-a-Question

In Office 2000, users had to run the Office Assistant (see the tip) to get answers to plain-English questions. In Office XP, however, this isn't the case. Simply do the following:

The Office Assistant is turned off by default. To turn it on, pull down the Help menu and click Show Office Assistant.

The Assistant is an animated (and frequently unpopular) helper which answers questions, but you can achieve the same effect more easily with Ask-a-Question.

Type in your question here and press Enter

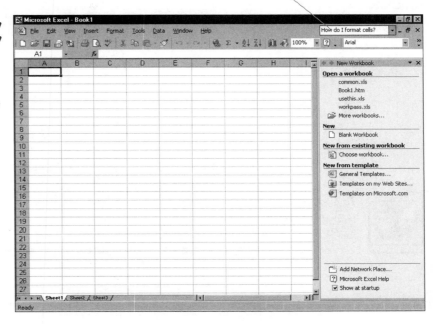

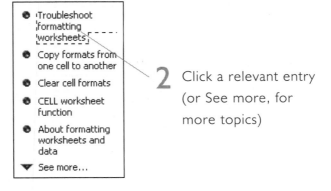

2 Click a relevant entry (or See more, for more topics)

Use the Contents and Index tabs as you would in any other

program.

3 Optional – click Show All to display all sub-topics

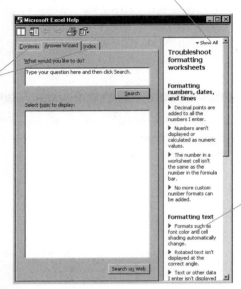

4 Or click an individual topic

To print out a topic, click this icon:

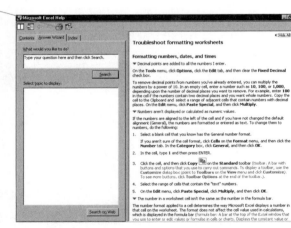

The result of step 3 – all the topics are enlarged (the expanded text is shown in green)

The Shortcut bar – an overview

Windows 98/ 2000/Me are an exception to this, in that you can create program buttons in the Quick Launch section of the Taskbar:

A button to start Word 2002 has been added...

However, the Shortcut bar is easier to use, and more convenient.

If the Shortcut bar isn't currently on-screen, do the following.
Click the Windows Start button. Then click Programs, Microsoft Office Tools, Microsoft Office Shortcut Bar.

The main function of the Windows Taskbar is to switch between already open applications. However, it doesn't let you start programs directly with a single click on a button (instead, you have to use the normal Start menu route, which requires several clicks and/or mouse movements). The Office Shortcut bar rectifies this omission. You can add buttons for any programs you want, and start them very quickly and easily.

The Shortcut bar also mimics the Taskbar, but with one important difference. If a program is already open, clicking on its button on the Shortcut bar switches to it and also opens a new blank window. (This only works with Office XP programs; if you try it with other applications, a second copy launches instead.)

You can determine the Shortcut bar's on-screen location. Additionally, you can have it display permanently, or 'auto-hide' it (where it only appears on screen when you move the mouse pointer to a specific screen area).

Toolbars

Buttons on the Shortcut bar are organised into specialist *toolbars*. The main ones are:

Office	has buttons relating specifically to Office XP modules
Programs	has buttons representing program folders
Desktop	has buttons representing items on your Desktop (e.g. My Computer, Internet Explorer and Recycle Bin)
Accessories	has buttons representing programs normally accessed from the Start/Accessories menu (e.g. Notepad, WordPad and Paint)
Favorites	has links to Web (and other) sites you've designated as Favorites

You can display as many, or as few, toolbars as you want.

Displaying Shortcut bar toolbars

Only three of the available toolbars are currently displaying – see 'Hiding/revealing toolbars' below for how to remedy this.

Office uses a unique effect when you have more than one toolbar displayed at once on the Shortcut bar: it *layers* them.

Look at the illustration below:

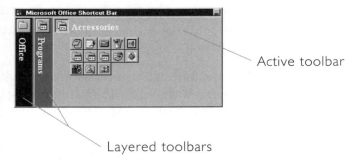

Active toolbar

Here, the Shortcut bar is 'floating'; for how to display it on the top, bottom, left or right of your screen instead, see the facing page.

Layered toolbars

To make another toolbar active, simply left-click on it.

Hiding/revealing toolbars

To display a toolbar, move the mouse pointer over the Shortcut bar and right-click once. Now do the following:

To hide a toolbar, click its entry – the tick disappears.

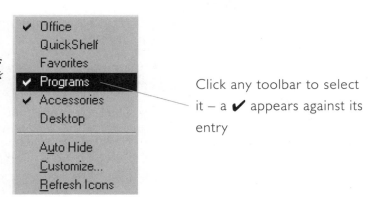

Click any toolbar to select it – a ✔ appears against its entry

Repeat this procedure for however many toolbars you want to hide or reveal.

Specifying the Shortcut bar location

You can have the Shortcut bar display on the left or right, or on the top or bottom of your screen. Alternatively, you can have it 'float' on screen, as a separate window. Use whichever method is most convenient for the task in hand.

Positioning the Shortcut bar on the screen edge

To move the Shortcut bar to the top, bottom, left or right of your screen (Office calls this 'docking'), place the mouse pointer anywhere over the Shortcut bar (but not over one of the buttons). Hold down the left mouse button and drag the bar to the appropriate area. When you release the button, the bar 'docks' automatically.

To turn on multiple language editing, click the Windows Start button. Select Programs, Microsoft Office Tools, Microsoft Office XP Language Settings. In the dialog, select an installed Office version, then the new language(s) you want to use. Click Add followed by OK.

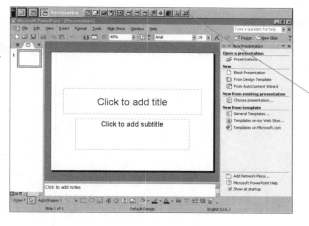

The Shortcut bar positioned horizontally over PowerPoint

Restoring the Shortcut bar to its previous location

Double-click its Title bar

Auto-hiding the Shortcut bar

For more information on how to interact with the Shortcut bar when it's floating, see your Windows documentation.

When it's floating, the Shortcut bar behaves much like any other window. For example, if it's minimised, clicking on the Shortcut bar button on the Taskbar:

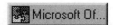

maximises it.

If it's docked, though, the Shortcut bar can be made to conceal itself when not required (this is called Auto-Hide). To do this, double-click in the Shortcut bar (but *not* on a button, or in the Title bar). Now do the following:

You can also use a shortcut to Auto-Hide the Shortcut bar.

Right-click over the bar; in the menu which appears, click Auto Hide. (This procedure also revokes Auto-Hide, if required.)

Ensure the View tab is active

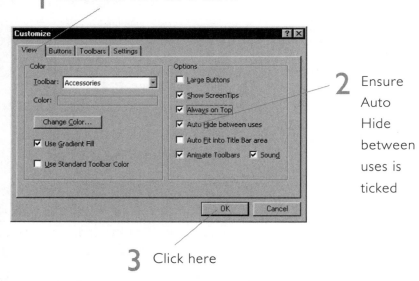

2 Ensure Auto Hide between uses is ticked

3 Click here

If the Shortcut bar is floating (not docked), Auto-Hide has no immediate effect on it.

Making the Shortcut bar reappear temporarily

To make the Shortcut bar visible again when you need it, simply move the mouse pointer to the edge of the screen where the Office Shortcut bar is docked. For instance, if the bar was docked on the bottom of the screen, move the pointer as far down as it will go.

When you've finished, move the mouse pointer away from the docking area; the Shortcut bar disappears again.

Adding buttons to the Shortcut bar

You can add buttons that represent files to the Shortcut bar. These files can be program files, or just about any other kind of file.

Double-click in the Shortcut bar (but *not* on a button, or in the Title bar). Now do the following:

| Ensure this tab is active   2 Click here; select a toolbar

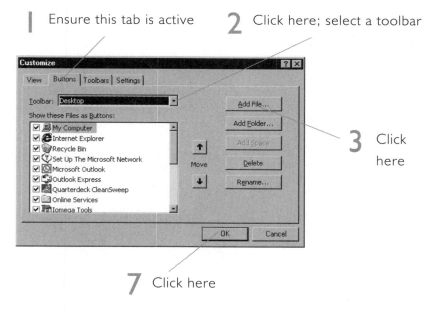

3 Click here

7 Click here

4 Click here. In the drop-down list, click the relevant drive/folder combination

Here, a button for Word 2002 is being added to the Shortcut bar.

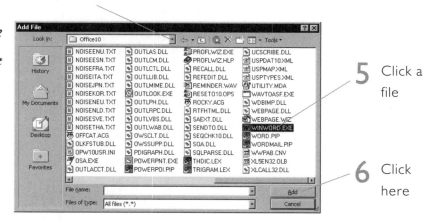

5 Click a file

6 Click here

Quick File Switching

In the past, only programs (not individual windows within programs) displayed on the Windows Taskbar. With Office XP, however, all open windows display as separate buttons.

In the following example, four new documents have been created in Word 2002. All four display as separate windows, although only one copy of Word 2002 is running:

Four Word 2002 windows

This is clarified by a glance at Word 2002's Window menu which (as before) shows all open Word windows:

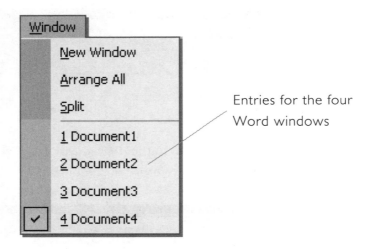

Entries for the four Word windows

Use this technique to go to a document window by simply clicking its Taskbar button, a considerable saving in time and effort.

Repairing errors

Office XP provides a special feature you can use to repair damage to modules.

Detect and Repair

Do the following to correct program errors (but note selecting Discard my customised settings and restore default settings in step 2 will ensure that all default Office settings are restored, so any you've customised – including menu/toolbar position, new Shortcut Bar buttons and view settings – will be lost):

1 In any module, pull down the Help menu and select Detect and Repair

2 Select one or both options

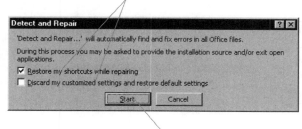

3 Click here

4 Follow the on-screen instructions – Detect and Repair can be a lengthy process

5 You may have to re-enter your user name and initials when you restart your Office applications

You can also use a further procedure for instances when an Office module 'hangs' (ceases to respond).

Application Recovery

When errors occur, Word, Excel and PowerPoint should give you the option of saving open files before the application closes.

1 Click Start, Programs, Microsoft Office Tools, Microsoft Office Application Recovery

2 Select the program which isn't responding

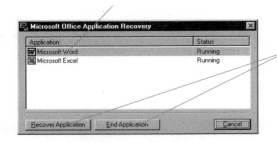

3 Click Recover Application to have Office try to recover the file(s) you were working on, or End Application to close the module with data loss

Re step 5 – files with [Recovered] against them are usually more recent than those with [Original] in the title.

(An alternative approach – you may find it useful to view all file versions and save the best.)

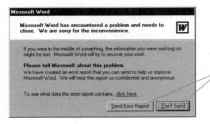

4 Select Send Error Report to email error details to Microsoft, or Don't Send

This is the Document Recovery Task Pane – when you've finished with it, click Close:

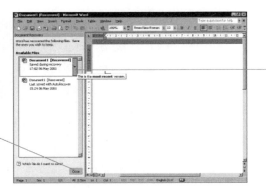

5 Open the application. Click the file you want to keep (usually the most recent). In the menu, select Open or View to view it or Save As to save it

Install on Demand

To subscribe to a document on a server running Office Server Extensions, first open it. Pull down the Tools menu and click Online Collaboration, Web Discussions. (If necessary, select a discussion server in the Discussion Options dialog and click OK.) In the Discussions toolbar, click the Subscribe button.

Now follow the on-screen instructions.

The Office XP applications make use of a feature which allows users to install programs and program components on demand, only when they're needed. The following display within the host programs:

- shortcuts

- icons

- menu entries

for the uninstalled features.

An example of Install on Demand is themes. By default, only a few themes are copied to the user's hard disk. When you attempt to apply a theme which hasn't been installed, you're invited to rectify this. Do the following:

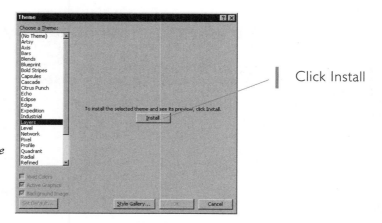

Click Install

To add a theme to a Word file, click Theme in the Format menu. Carry out step 1 (and 2, if required). Click OK.

After a pause, step 1 typically produces a further dialog. Insert the requested Office XP CD and carry out step 2:

Networked users may be asked to refer to a specific server location instead...

2 Click here

Collect and Paste

You can copy multiple items to the Office Clipboard from within any Windows program which supports copy-and-paste, but you can only paste in the last one (except in Office modules).

Using Office XP, if you want to copy-and-paste multiple items of text and/or pictures into a document, you can now copy as many as 24 items. These are stored in a special version of the Windows Clipboard called the Office Clipboard, which in turn is located in the Task Pane. The Office Clipboard displays a visual representation of the data.

Using the Office Clipboard

From within Word, Excel, PowerPoint or Outlook, use standard procedures to copy multiple examples of text and/or pictures – after the first copy, the Clipboard appears in the Task Pane. Do the following, in the same or another module:

To clear the contents of the Office XP Clipboard, click Clear All.

1 Click the data you want to insert – it appears at the insertion point

To call up the Office Clipboard at any time, pull down the Edit menu and click Office Clipboard.

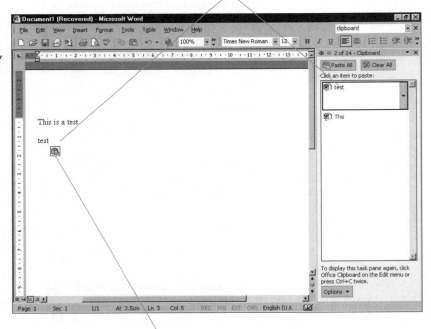

Copying items bigger than 4Mb (with up to 64 Mb of RAM) or 8Mb (with more than 64Mb) to the Office Clipboard will mean it can accept no further data.

2 A Smart Tag appears – see chapter 2

Office's Task Pane

The New Document Task Pane is called the New Workbook and New Presentation Task Pane in Excel and PowerPoint respectively. (It's also slightly different in each.)

Office XP modules provide a special pane on the right of the screen which you can use to launch various tasks or apply specific formatting. There are various incarnations of the Task Pane, depending on which module you're using. For example, Word 2002 has eight, of which the main ones are:

- New Document (see page 14)

- Clipboard (see the facing page)

- Search (see chapter 2)

- Insert Clip Art (see chapter 2)

There are also specific formatting versions which are discussed in chapter 2.

Using the Task Pane

To display or hide the Task Pane, see the DON'T FORGET tip on page 9. (You can also use a menu route: pull down the View menu and click Task Pane.)

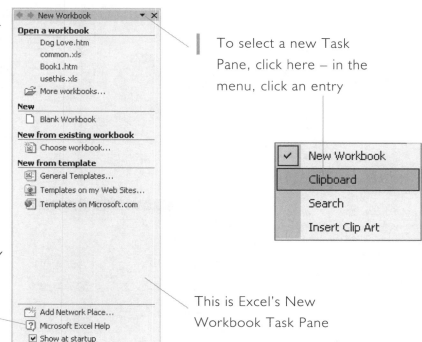

To select a new Task Pane, click here – in the menu, click an entry

This is Excel's New Workbook Task Pane

In the New Document, New Workbook or New Presentation Task Pane, click here: to launch HELP.

Digital signatures

You can attach digital signatures to Office XP documents, as a way of enhancing security. The signature confirms that the document was sent by you and hasn't been altered in any way, and uses a digital certificate.

Creating digital certificates

You can also obtain digital certificates from commercial companies. For more information, visit:

http://officeupdate. microsoft.com/office/ redirect/10/Helplinks.asp

Follow the on-screen instructions

1 | Locate a file called SELFCERT.EXE (usually in the C:\Program Files\Microsoft Office\Office10\ folder)

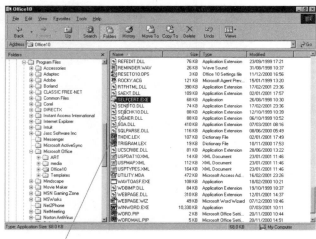

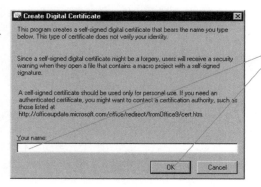

Running the procedure here creates a self-certification. Self-certification doesn't carry the weight of certification by a formal certification authority (see the above tip).

2 Double-click SELFCERT.EXE

3 Enter your name and confirm

...cont'd

Applying digital signatures

If you're using Office as a member of an organisation, it may have its own certification authority. Contact your network administrator or IT department for more information.

1 In Word, Excel or PowerPoint, pull down the Tools menu and click Options.

2 Click the Security tab

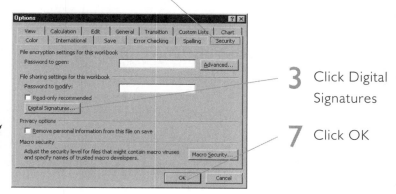

3 Click Digital Signatures

7 Click OK

Digitally signing documents may have no legal validity.

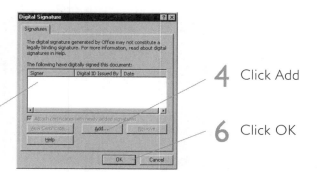

To remove a digital signature, select it here and click

Remove.

4 Click Add

6 Click OK

You can only apply signatures to files which have been saved (Office reminds you if this isn't the case).
By the same token, saving a file after you've signed it removes the signature.

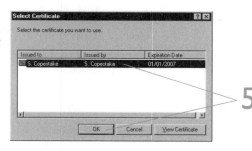

5 Select a certificate and confirm

Document imaging

Re step 1 – to scan in documents instead, click File, Scan New Document. Complete the Microsoft Office Document Scanning dialog (e.g. select a preset according to the type of document). Click Scan.

The results of the OCR conversion can sometimes be less than impressive.

To save file details, pull down the File menu and click Save.

To see file details, pull down the File menu and click Properties.

View the tabs for details

OCR data – click OK when you've finished

Office has a special utility which lets you work with text or TIF images in faxes or scanned files. By using Document Imaging, you can:

- scan in new documents or open existing TIF files

- extract the text from TIF files (using OCR – Optical Character Recognition) and (optionally) export it to Word

- read scanned files easily on-screen

Using document imaging

1 Click Start, Programs, Microsoft Office Tools, Microsoft Office Document Imaging

2 Click File, Open – use the Open dialog to locate and open a fax or TIF file

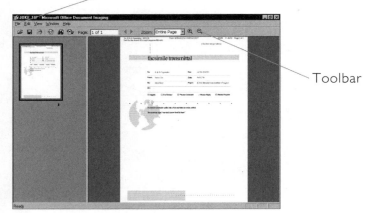

Toolbar

3 Change the view by clicking in the Zoom field in the toolbar and selecting a new zoom

4 To extract the text, choose File, Recognize Text Using OCR. (To export it into a new Word document, choose File, Send Text to Word – Word opens a new document containing the text)

Word 2002

Here, you'll become familiar with basic/advanced Word use. You'll enter/select text, send e-mail and use Smart Tags. You'll format text, translate it and use styles. Finally, you'll proof/summarise your work; create bookmarks/hyperlinks; insert images, Web backgrounds/watermarks; customise page layout/printing; and handwrite text.

Covers

Chapter Two

The Word 2002 screen

Below is a detailed illustration of the Word 2002 screen:

Title bar   Menu bar

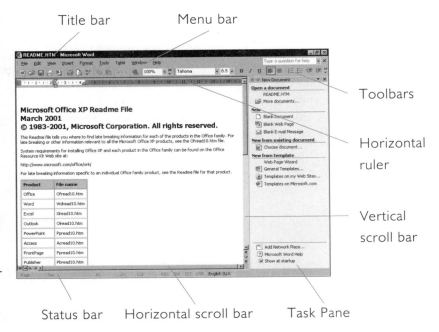

Toolbars

Horizontal ruler

Vertical scroll bar

Status bar   Horizontal scroll bar   Task Pane

The Status bar displays information relating to the active document (e.g. what page you're on).

Some of these – e.g. the rulers and scroll bars – are standard to just about all programs that run under Windows. Many of them can be hidden, if required.

Specifying which screen components display

Pull down the Tools menu and click Options. Then:

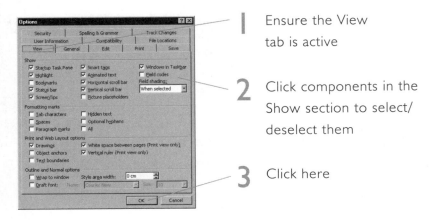

1 Ensure the View tab is active

2 Click components in the Show section to select/deselect them

3 Click here

Entering text

Word 2002 lets you enter text immediately after you've started it (you can do this because a new blank document is automatically created based on the default template). In Word, you enter text at the insertion point:

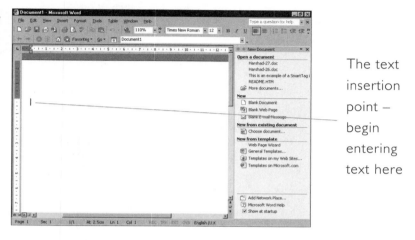

The text insertion point — begin entering text here

Additional characters

Most of the text you need to enter can be typed in directly from the keyboard. However, it's sometimes necessary to enter special characters, e.g. bullets (for instance: ✍) or special symbols like ©.

Pull down the Insert menu and click Symbol. Do the following:

1 Ensure the Symbols tab is active

2 Click here; select the appropriate font from the list

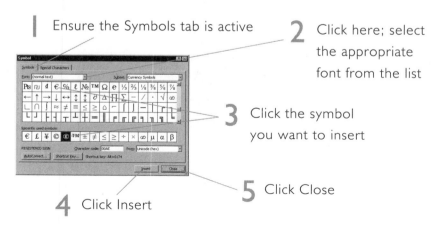

3 Click the symbol you want to insert

4 Click Insert

5 Click Close

Selecting text

Word 2002 supports standard Windows text selection techniques. However, it also supports the following:

Selecting partial text blocks

To select a rectangular portion of 1 or more paragraphs, hold down Alt as you drag with the mouse

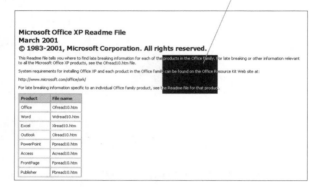

Selecting multiple text blocks

To select more than 1 text block, hold down Ctrl+Shift as you drag with the mouse

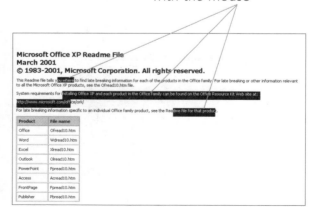

Click and Type

You can also enter text in a special way in Word 2002, one that makes the process much easier. With Click and Type:

- you can enter text or pictures in most blank page areas, with the minimum of mouse activity

- you don't have to apply the necessary formatting yourself – Word 2002 does this automatically (e.g. you can insert text to the right of an existing paragraph without having to insert manual tab stops)

Using Click and Type

In Web Layout or Print Layout view, position the mouse pointer where you want to insert text or a picture. Click once – the pointer changes to indicate the formatting which Word 2002 will apply:

If Click and Type isn't enabled, pull down the Tools menu and click Options. In the Options dialog, activate the Edit tab. In the Click and type section, tick Enable click and type. Click OK.

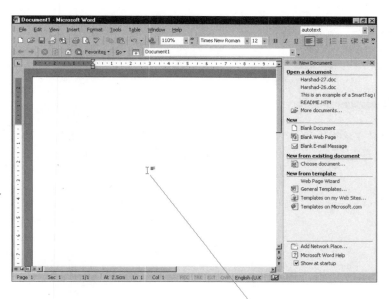

Here, the pointer shows that Word 2002 is about to left-align new text...

Now double-click, then do the following:

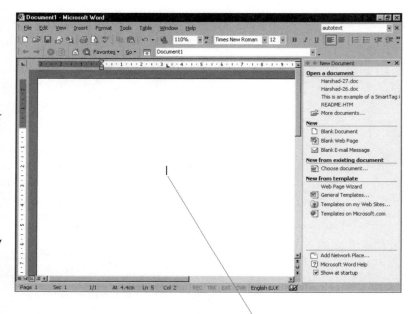

 If you use Click and Type beneath an existing text paragraph, Word 2002 applies a specific style to the new text. You can specify the style used.

Pull down the Tools menu and click Options. In the Options dialog, activate the Edit tab. In the Click and type section, click in this field:

In the drop-down list, select a style. Finally, click OK.

Begin entering text, or insert a picture in the normal way

The Click and Type pointers

The main pointers are:

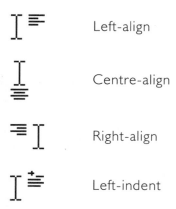

Left-align

Centre-align

Right-align

Left-indent

Using Smart Tags

You can disable Smart Tags. In the Tools menu click AutoCorrect Options. In the dialog, select the Smart Tags tab. Untick Label text with smart tags.

Word 2002 recognises certain types of data and underlines them with a dotted purple underline or a small blue box. When you move the mouse pointer over the line/box an 'action button' appears which provides access to commands which would otherwise have to be accessed from menus/ toolbars or other programs.

The Paste Options button

Re step 2 – choose Keep Source Formatting to retain the pasted text's original format, or Match Destination Formatting to make it conform to the host text.

'Button' has been copied and the Paste command (Shift+Insert) issued...

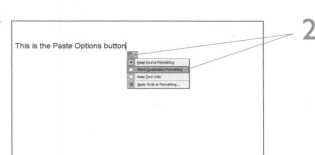

2 Clicking the arrow launches a menu – make a choice

Types of data Word applies Smart Tags to include the following:

- *dates/times*
- *places/addresses*
- *Outlook email recipients*

Options for a date Smart Tag

The AutoCorrect button

An AutoCorrect entry has been set up which replaces 'bu' with 'button'

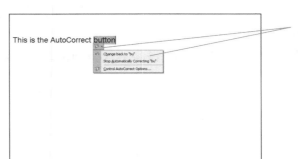

2 Clicking the arrow launches a menu – make a choice

Here, you can opt to have the AutoCorrect correction undone just this once ('Change back to "bu"') or you can stop the correction being made in future ('Stop automatically correcting "bu"').

Sending e-mail

To send e-mail from Word, you must have specified Outlook 2002 as your Internet e-mail program.

Within Internet Explorer, click Internet Options in the Tools menu. Click the Programs tab. In the E-mail field, select Microsoft Outlook. Click OK.

You can use Word to write and send e-mail messages (provided you've also installed Outlook).

In the New Document Task Pane, click General Templates. In the New dialog, activate the General tab. Double-click the E-mail Message icon. Now do the following:

| Type in the recipient's e-mail address

2 Type in a subject

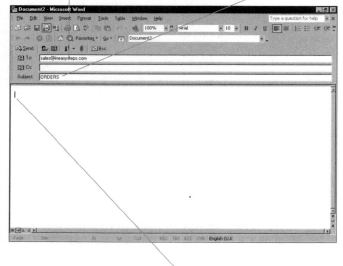

If you want to send a copy (or copies) of the e-mail to other recipients, also complete the Cc ('Carbon' or 'Courtesy' copy) section.

3 Type in your message

4 Click this toolbar button:

You may have to configure Outlook 2002's Remote Mail facility before you can send e-mail. See chapter 6.

E-mailing a pre-written document

| Click this button in Word's Standard toolbar:

2 Follow steps 1, 2 and 4 above

Moving around in documents

To move to the location where you last made an amendment, press Shift+F5.
You can do this as many as three times in succession.

You can use the following to move through Word 2002 documents:

- keystrokes

- the vertical/horizontal scroll bars

- the Go To section of the Find and Replace dialog

The keystroke route

Word implements the standard Windows direction keys. Use the left, right, up and down cursor keys in the usual way. Additionally, Home, End, Page Up and Page Down work normally.

The scroll bar route

Use your mouse to perform any of the following actions:

When you drag the box on the vertical scroll bar, Word 2002 displays a page indicator showing which page you're up to.
(The page indicator doesn't appear in Web Layout view.)

Click anywhere here to jump to another location in the document

Click anywhere here to jump to another location in the document

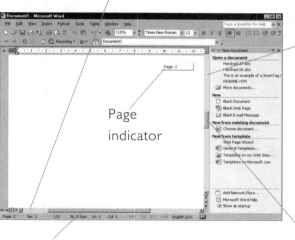

Page indicator

Drag this to the left or right to extend the viewing area

Drag this up or down to move through the active document

You can use a keyboard shortcut to launch the Go To dialog: simply press Ctrl+G.

The dialog route

You can use the Go To tab in the Find and Replace dialog to move to a variety of document locations. These include:

- pages (probably the most common)

- lines

- pictures

Pull down the Edit menu and click Go To. Now do the following:

To have Word count the words in the active document, pull down the Tools menu and click Word Count. This is the result:

| Click the location type you want to go to   3 Click here

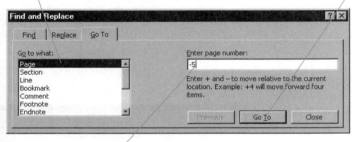

2 Type in the specific location reference (e.g. a number if you selected 'Page' in step 1)

There are some useful refinements:

- You can enter *relative* movements in step 2. For example, if you want to move seventeen pages back from the present location, type in -17. Or +5 to move five pages forward…

- To move to the next or previous instance of the specified location (i.e. without specifying a reference), omit step 2. In step 3, the dialog is now slightly different; click Next or Previous, as appropriate. Click Close when you've finished.

You can also launch a special Word Count toolbar. Click Show Toolbar:

Click here for more data

Views

Word 2002 also provides another view which you'll use frequently: Print Preview.

In Print Layout view, you can hide blank (unused) space. Move the mouse pointer over the top or bottom of the page – two white arrows appear. Click to toggle between hiding and displaying white space.

The stationery shown in the illustration can be found in the following folder:

Program Files\Common Files\Microsoft Shared\Stationery

(Viewing this file in Normal or Print Layout views restricts what you see.)

In Outlook, you can use stationeries to make e-mail more visually attractive (but only if you aren't using Word 2002 as your e-mail editor).

Word 2002 lets you examine your work in various ways, according to the approach you need. It calls these 'views'. The principal views are:

Normal

Normal View – the default – is used for basic text editing. In Normal View, text formatting elements are still visible; for instance, coloured, emboldened or italicised text displays faithfully. However, little attempt is made to show document structure or layout (for example, headers/footers, page boundaries and most pictures are invisible). For these reasons, Normal View is quick and easy to use. It's suitable for bulk text entry and editing, but not recommended for use with graphics.

Print Layout

Print Layout view works like Normal view, with one exception: the positioning of items on the page is reproduced accurately. Headers/footers and pictures are visible, and can be edited directly; margins display faithfully.

In Print Layout view, the screen is updated more slowly. Use it when your document is nearing completion.

Web Layout

In Web layout view, Web pages are optimised so that they appear as they will when published to the Web or an Intranet. Effects which are often used on the Web display (e.g. backgrounds and AutoShapes).

Word 2002 displaying one of Outlook's HTML stationeries

When Full Screen view is active, you lose access to toolbars and scroll bars. However, you should still be able to access the menus by using the keyboard (e.g. Alt+F to launch the File menu).

Full Screen

Unless you have a particularly large monitor, you'll probably find that there are times when your screen is too cluttered. Full Screen view hides all standard screen components in one operation, thereby making more space available for editing.

Use Full Screen view when you need it, as an adjunct to Normal or Print Layout view.

Summarising documents

Summarizing – as part of Office XP's Install on Demand – may not be installed. If it isn't, Word launches a special message. Follow the on-screen instructions.

In effect, Word provides another way to view a document: you can 'summarise' it. When you summarise a document, Word 2002:

- analyses it and allocates a 'score' to each sentence
- allocates a higher score for sentences which contain repeated words

After this, you specify what percentage of the higher-scoring sentences you want to display.

To switch to another view, pull down the View menu and select one (but see below).

To summarise the active document, pull down the Tools menu and click AutoSummarize. Word 2002 carries out the initial analysis. When it's completed, do the following:

To leave Full Screen view, press Esc or do the following in the on-screen toolbar:

Click here

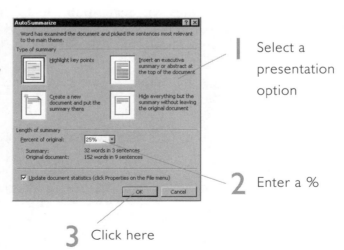

1 Select a presentation option

2 Enter a %

3 Click here

Changing zoom levels

The ability to vary the level of magnification for the active document is often useful. Sometimes, it's helpful to 'zoom out' (i.e. decrease the magnification) so that you can take an overview; at other times, you'll need to 'zoom in' (increase the magnification) to work in greater detail. Word 2002 lets you do either of these very easily.

You can do any of the following:

- choose from preset zoom levels (e.g. 100%, 75%)

- specify your own zoom percentage

- choose Many Pages, to view a specific number of pages

Setting the zoom level

The Zoom dialog varies slightly according to which view you're using.

Pull down the View menu and click Zoom. Now carry out steps 1 or 2 (to specify a zoom %) OR 3 & 4 (to specify a group of pages). Finally, in either case, follow step 5.

| Click a preset zoom level

The Preview section provides an indication of what the selected view level looks like.

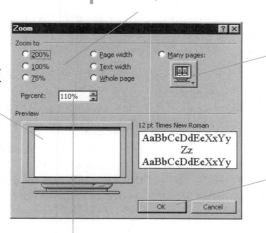

3 Click here (this option is unavailable in Normal and Web Layout views)

5 Click here

Re step 2 – entries here must lie in the following range: 10%-500%.

2 Type in your own zoom percentage

4 Click a multiple-page view

Formatting text – an overview

Word 2002 lets you format text in a variety of ways. Broadly, however, text formatting can be divided into two overall categories:

You can have Word 2002 format the active document automatically.

Pull down the Tools menu and click AutoCorrect. In the AutoCorrect dialog, click the AutoFormat tab. Specify the type(s) of formatting you want applied. Finally, click OK.

Character formatting

Character formatting is concerned with altering the *appearance* of selected text. Examples include:

* changing the font and type size

* colouring text

* changing the font style (bold, italic etc.)

* underlining text

* applying font effects (superscript, subscript, small caps etc.)

Character formatting is a misnomer in one sense: it can also be applied to specific paragraphs of text.

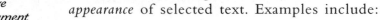

Note that whenever you type in Internet paths – for instance:

http://www.ineasysteps.com

AutoFormat automatically implements them as hypertext links. This means that clicking an address takes you there (if your Internet link is currently open).

(If you want to turn this feature off, pull down the Tools menu and select AutoCorrect Options. In the dialog, select the AutoFormat As You Type tab. Untick Internet and network paths with hyperlinks. Click OK.)

Paragraph formatting

Paragraph formatting has to do with the structuring and layout of paragraphs of text. Examples include:

* specifying paragraph indents

* specifying paragraph alignment (e.g. left or right justification)

* specifying paragraph and line spacing

* imposing borders and/or fills on paragraphs

The term "paragraph formatting" is also something of a misnomer in that some of these – for instance, line-spacing – can also be applied to the whole of the active document rather than selected paragraphs.

Changing the font or type size

Character formatting can be changed in two ways:

- from within the Font dialog

- (to a lesser extent) by using the Formatting toolbar

Applying a new font/type size – the dialog route

First, select the text whose typeface and/or type size you want to amend. Pull down the Format menu and click Font. Now carry out step 1. Perform step 2 and/or 3. Finally, carry out step 4:

Ensure the Font tab is active

Re step 3 – as well as whole point sizes, you can also enter half-point increments. For instance, Word 2002 will accept 10, 10.5 or 11 but not 10.7 or 10.85.

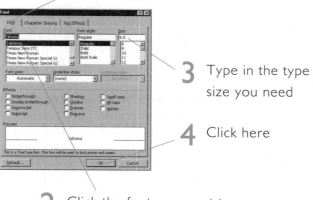

3 Type in the type size you need

4 Click here

2 Click the font you want to use

If the Formatting toolbar isn't currently visible, pull down the View menu and click Toolbars, Formatting.

Applying a new font/type size – the toolbar route

Make sure the Formatting toolbar is visible. Now select the text you want to amend and do the following:

Click here; select the font you want to use in the drop-down list

Type in the type size you need and press Enter

Changing text colour

You can also change font styles. The default font style is Regular. Additional font styles depend on the typeface. For example, 'Times New Roman' has 'Bold', 'Italic' and 'Bold Italic' while 'Arial Rounded MT Bold' merely has 'Bold' and 'Bold Italic'. Select a font style here:

First, select the text you want to alter. Pull down the Format menu and click Font. Now do the following:

Ensure the Font tab is active

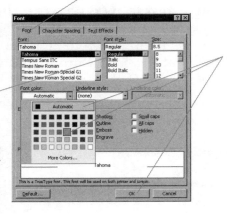

2 Click here, select a colour then confirm

Don't confuse font styles with text styles (text styles are groups of formatting commands and are much more diverse – see pages 71-74).

Verifying current text formatting

If you're in any doubt about what character/paragraph formatting attributes are associated with text, press Shift+F1. Now click in the text. This is the result:

Re step 2 – clicking Automatic sets the colour to black (unless you've amended the default Windows text colour).

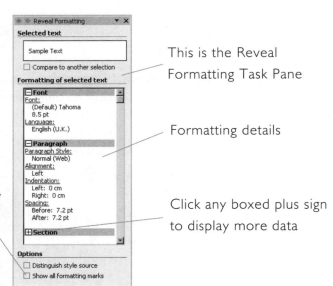

This is the Reveal Formatting Task Pane

Formatting details

Click any boxed plus sign to display more data

Select Show all formatting marks to display tabs, paragraph marks and spaces etc. within the document.

Font effects

The following are the principal font effects:

- Strikethrough – e.g. ~~font effect~~

- Superscript – e.g. f$^{\text{ont effect}}$

- Subscript – e.g. f$_{\text{ont effect}}$

- All Caps – e.g. FONT EFFECT

- Small Caps – e.g. FONT EFFECT

You can also use the following handy keyboard shortcuts:

Ctrl++	*Superscript*
Ctrl+=	*Subscript*
Ctrl+Shift+K	*Small Caps*
Ctrl+Shift+A	*All Caps*
Ctrl+Shift+H	*Hidden*

In addition, you can mark text as hidden, which means that it doesn't display on screen or print.

Applying font effects

First, select the relevant text. Pull down the Format menu and click Font. Then carry out the following steps:

Ensure the Font tab is active

Many of the font effects can be combined – e.g. Superscript with Small Caps. However, Small Caps and All Caps are mutually exclusive.

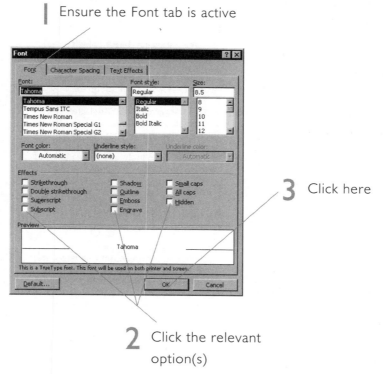

3 Click here

2 Click the relevant option(s)

Indenting paragraphs – an overview

Indents are a crucial component of document layout. For instance, in most document types, indenting the first line of paragraphs (i.e. moving it inwards away from the left page margin) makes the text much more legible.

You can achieve a similar effect by using tabs. However, indents are easier to apply (and amend subsequently).

Other document types – e.g. bibliographies – can use the following:

- negative indents (where the direction of indent is towards and beyond the left margin)

- hanging indents (where the first line is unaltered, while subsequent lines are indented)

- full indents (where the entire paragraph is indented away from the left and/or the right margins)

Don't confuse indents with page margins. Margins are the gap between the edge of the page and the text area; indents define the distance between the margins and text.

Some of the potential indent combinations are shown in the illustration below:

This paragraph has a full left and right indent. It's best, however, not to overdo the extent of the indent: 0.35 inches is often more than adequate.

left & right indent

This paragraph has a first-line indent. This type of indent is suitable for most document types. It's best, however, not to overdo the extent of the indent: 0.35 inches is often more than adequate.

first-line indent

This paragraph has a negative left indent. It's best, however, not to overdo the extent of the indent: 0.35 inches is often more than adequate.

negative left indent

This paragraph has a hanging indent. It's best, however, not to overdo the extent of the indent: 0.35 inches is often more than adequate.

hanging indent

Left margin (inserted for illustration purposes)

Right margin (inserted for illustration purposes)

Applying indents to paragraphs

Indenting text – the dialog route

Select the paragraph(s) you want to indent. Pull down the Format menu and click Paragraph. Follow step 1 below. If you want a left indent, carry out step 2. For a right indent, follow step 3. To achieve a first-line or hanging indent, follow step 4. Finally, carry out step 5.

Ensure the Indents and Spacing tab is active

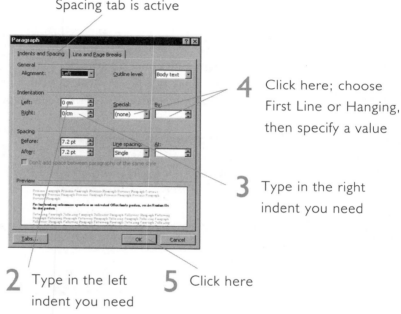

4 Click here; choose First Line or Hanging, then specify a value

3 Type in the right indent you need

Re steps 2 and 3 – type in minus values for negative indents.

2 Type in the left indent you need

5 Click here

If the Formatting toolbar isn't visible, pull down the View menu and click Toolbars, Formatting.

Indenting text – the toolbar route

First, select the relevant paragraph(s). Ensure the Formatting toolbar is visible. Then click one of these:

Increases the indent

Using the Formatting toolbar route provides fewer indent options.

Decreases the indent

Aligning paragraphs

Word 2002 supports the following types of alignment:

Left alignment
Text is flush with the left page margin.

Right alignment
Text is flush with the right page margin.

Justification
Text is flush with the left *and* right page margins.

Centred
Text is placed evenly between the left/right page margins.

Re the HOT TIP below – if you've used the Right Align or Justify buttons before, Word 2002 may have promoted them to the main body of the Formatting toolbar.

To right-align or justify the selected text, click this button on the right of the toolbar:

In the flyout, click one of these:

Right-align

Justify

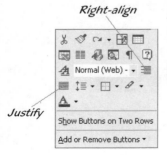

Aligning text – the dialog route

First, select the paragraph(s) you want to align. Pull down the Format menu and click Paragraph. Now:

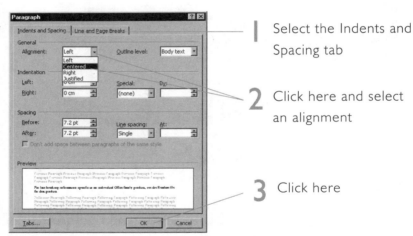

1 Select the Indents and Spacing tab

2 Click here and select an alignment

3 Click here

Aligning text – the toolbar route

Select the relevant paragraph(s). Then click one of these:

Left align   Centre

Specifying paragraph spacing

As a general rule, set low paragraph spacing settings: a little goes a long way.

Word 2002 lets you customise the vertical space before and/ or after specific text paragraphs. This is a useful device for increasing text legibility.

By default, Word defines paragraph spacing – like type sizes – in point sizes. However, if you want you can enter measurements in different units. To do this, apply any of the following suffixes to values you enter:

- in – for inches (e.g. '2 in')

- cm – for centimetres (e.g. '5 cm')

- pi – for picas (e.g. '14 pi')

- px – for pixels (e.g. '40 px' – about ½ inch)

You should find the following typographical/ computing definitions useful:

- *Picas are an alternative measure in typography: one pica is almost equivalent to one-sixth inch. Picas are often used to define line length*

- *Pixels (a contraction of 'picture elements') are the smallest components of the picture on a computer monitor*

Applying paragraph spacing

First, select the paragraph you want to indent. Pull down the Format menu and click Paragraph. Now carry out the steps below:

1 Ensure the Indents and Spacing tab is active

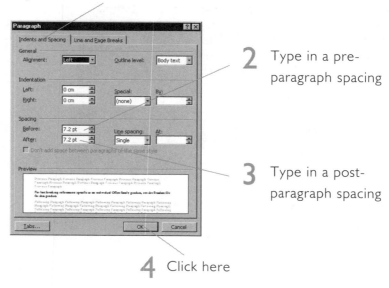

2 Type in a pre-paragraph spacing

3 Type in a post-paragraph spacing

4 Click here

Adjusting line spacing

Line spacing (also known as leading – pronounced 'ledding') is the vertical distance between individual lines of text.

You can apply the following types of leading:

- *Single – each line of type is separated by an amount slightly greater than the type size. This is the default*

- *1.5 Lines – 150% of single line spacing*

- *Double – 200% of single line spacing*

- *At Least – sets the minimum line height at the value you specify*

- *Exactly – sets the value you specify as an unvarying line height: Word 2002 cannot adjust it*

- *Multiple – sets line height as a multiple of single-spaced text. (For example, specifying '3.5' here initiates a line height of 3.5 lines)*

You can use these keyboard shortcuts to adjust line spacing:

Ctrl+1	*Single spacing*
Ctrl+5	*1 ½ spacing*
Ctrl+2	*Double spacing*

First, select the relevant paragraph(s). Then move the mouse pointer over them and right-click. Do the following:

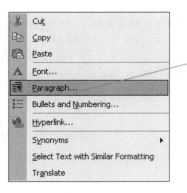

Click here (you can also use this technique to set the line spacing before you begin to enter text)

Now perform step 1 below. If you want to apply a preset spacing, follow step 2. To implement your own spacing, carry out steps 3 and 4 instead. Finally, follow step 5:

1 Ensure the Indents and Spacing tab is active

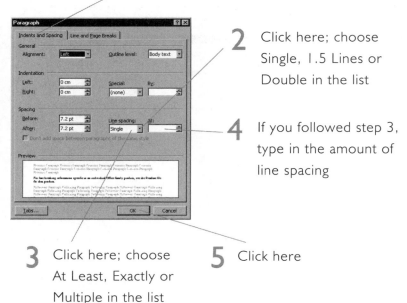

2 Click here; choose Single, 1.5 Lines or Double in the list

4 If you followed step 3, type in the amount of line spacing

3 Click here; choose At Least, Exactly or Multiple in the list

5 Click here

Paragraph borders

By default, Word 2002 does not border paragraph text. However, you can apply a wide selection of borders if you want. You can specify:

You can also border selected text within a paragraph. However, the Borders tab is then slightly different (e.g. you can't deselect the border for specific sides).

- the type and thickness of the border
- how many sides the border should have
- the border colour
- whether the text is shadowed or in 3-D
- the distance of the border from the text

Applying a border

First, select the paragraph(s) you want to border. Then pull down the Format menu and click Borders and Shading. Carry out step 1 below. Now carry out steps 2-5, as appropriate. Finally, perform step 6:

To set the distance from the border to the enclosed text, click Options. Insert the relevant distances and click OK. Then follow step 6.

1 Ensure the Borders tab is active

4 Click a border option to border all four sides of the text

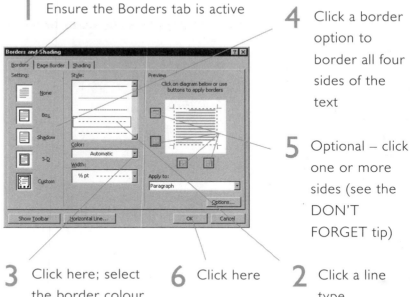

5 Optional – click one or more sides (see the DON'T FORGET tip)

Use step 5 to deselect the top, bottom, left or right paragraph borders. If you want to deselect more than one, repeat step 5 as often as necessary.

3 Click here; select the border colour from the drop-down list

6 Click here

2 Click a line type

Paragraph fills

By default, Word 2002 does not apply a fill to text paragraphs. However, you can do the following if you want:

- specify a percentage fill e.g. 20% (light grey) or 85% (very dark grey)

- apply a simple pattern, if required

- specify a background fill colour

- specify a pattern colour

Applying a fill

First, select the paragraph(s) you want to fill. Then pull down the Format menu and click Borders and Shading. Now carry out step 1 below. Follow steps 2, 3 or 4 as appropriate. Finally, carry out step 5:

Re steps 3 and 4 – you can achieve unique blends by applying different pattern and background colours.

1 Ensure the Shading tab is active

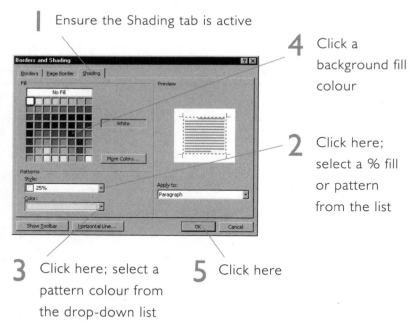

4 Click a background fill colour

2 Click here; select a % fill or pattern from the list

3 Click here; select a pattern colour from the drop-down list

5 Click here

Working with tabs

Tabs are a means of indenting the first line of text paragraphs (you can also use indents for this purpose – see pages 54-55).

pages 54-55

When you press the Tab key while the text-insertion point is at the start of a paragraph, the text in the first line jumps to the next tab stop – see the illustration below:

Never use the Space Bar to indent paragraphs: spaces vary in size according to the typeface and type size applying to specific paragraphs, and therefore give uneven results.

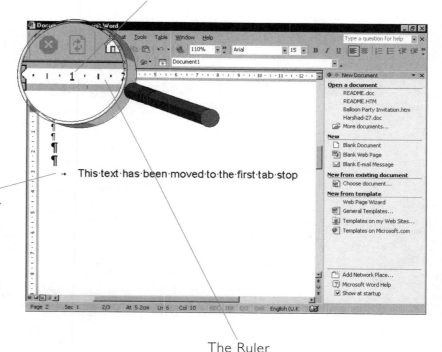

The first tab stop

The Ruler

The right-pointing arrow on the left of the text denotes the inserted tab.

To have tab stops (and other symbols) display, pull down the Tools menu and click Options. Activate the View tab, then select All in the Formatting marks section. Finally, click OK.

To display or hide the Ruler, pull down the View menu and click Ruler.

Inserting tabs is a useful way to increase the legibility of your text. By default, Word 2002 inserts tab stops automatically every half an inch. If you want, you can enter new or revised tab stop positions individually and with great precision.

Setting tab stops

First, select the paragraph(s) in which you need to set tab stops. Pull down the Format menu and click Tabs. Now carry out step 1 below. If you want to implement a new default tab stop position, follow step 2. If, on the other hand, you need to set up individual tab stops, carry out steps 3 AND 4 as often as necessary. Finally, in either case, follow step 5 to confirm your changes.

When you've performed steps 3 & 4, the individual tab stop position appears here:

2 Type in the new tab stop default (e.g. 0.35")

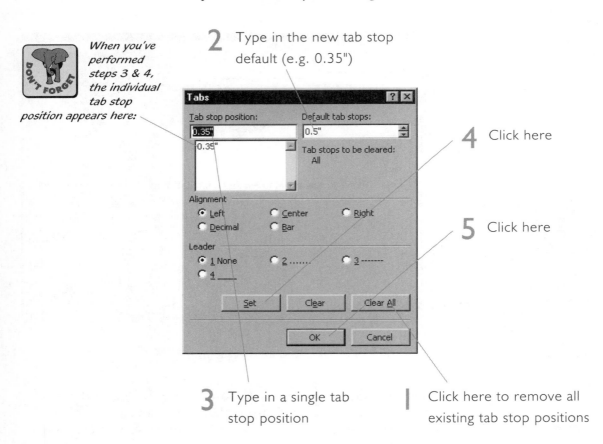

4 Click here

5 Click here

3 Type in a single tab stop position

1 Click here to remove all existing tab stop positions

Searching for text

Word 2002 lets you search for specific text within the active document. Even better, however, you can also search for character or paragraph formatting, either separately from the text search or at the same time.

For example, you can if you want have Word locate all instances of the word 'information'. Or you could have it find all italicised words, whatever they are. Similarly, you could have it flag all instances of *'information'*.

You can also:

- limit the search to words which match the case of the text you specify (e.g. if you search for 'Man', Word will not flag 'man' or 'MAN')

- limit the search to whole words (e.g. if you search for 'nation', Word will not flag 'international')

- have Word search for word forms (e.g. if you look for 'began', Word will also stop at 'begin', 'begun' and 'beginning')

- have Word search for homophones (e.g. if you look for 'there', Word will flag 'their')

Initiating a text search

Pull down the Edit menu and click Find. Now do the following:

*Follow step 2 to locate specific formatting, then carry out the following procedure.
In the extended dialog which launches, click Format. Word 2002 launches a menu; click the relevant entry. Then complete the dialog which appears in the normal way. Finally, follow step 3 to begin the search.*

*To highlight all instances of the specified text, click here:
Select an area (e.g. Main Document) in the list then click Find All.*

| Type in the text you want to find

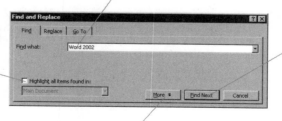

3 Click here to start the search

2 Optional – click More if the expanded form of the dialog isn't visible, then see the DON'T FORGET tip

Replacing text

Word 2002 replaces some words/phrases automatically as you type (e.g. 'accross' becomes 'across'). This is called AutoCorrect, and works with multiple languages (if you've set up Office to work with them – see page 25).

To add your own substitutions, pull down the Tools menu and click AutoCorrect. In the Replace field, insert the incorrect word; in the With field, type in the correct version. Click OK.

When you've located text and/or formatting, you can have Word 2002 replace it automatically with the text and/or formatting of your choice.

You can customise find-and-replace operations with the same parameters as a simple Find operation. For example, you can have Word find every occurrence of 'information' and replace it with *'information'*, or even *'data'*…

Initiating a find-and-replace operation

First pull down the Edit menu and click Replace. In the Find and Replace dialog, click More. Now follow steps 1 and 2 below. Carry out steps 3 and/or 4, as appropriate. Finally, follow either step 5 OR 6:

1 Type in the text you want to find

2 Type in the replacement text

5 Click here to replace the first instance of the specified text

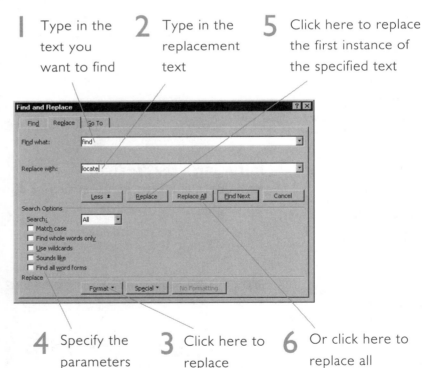

When you follow step 3, Word launches a menu; click the relevant entry. Then complete the dialog which appears in the normal way. Finally, carry out step 5 OR 6, as appropriate.

4 Specify the parameters you need

3 Click here to replace formatting

6 Or click here to replace all instances of the specified text

Searching via the Task Pane

If the Task Pane isn't visible, choose View, Task Pane.

You can use the Search Task Pane to search for files. You do this by entering text; Office then finds files which contain it.

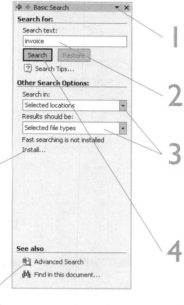

1 Click here; in the list, select Search

2 Type in the text you want to search for

3 Optional – specify a search directory and/ or limit the search to specific file types

4 Click Search

You can make the search process a lot faster by using fast searching. Click Install and follow the on-screen instructions.

For a more advanced search (for instance, you can specify AND/OR values), select Advanced Search before step 2.

5 Search returns a list of matches. To action one, click the arrow and select a menu option

To begin a new search, click Modify (this clears details of flagged files).

Working with headers and footers

To edit an existing header or footer, choose View, Header and Footer. Now click in the relevant header or footer and make any changes.

You can have Word 2002 print text at the top of each page within a document; this area is called the 'header'. In the same way, you can have text printed at the base of each page (the 'footer'). Headers and footers are printed within the top and bottom page margins, respectively.

When you create a header or footer, Word automatically switches the active document to Print Layout view and displays the Header and Footer toolbar.

Inserting a header

To insert a footer, follow step 1. Now click the following button in the toolbar:

Carry out steps 2-5 as appropriate.

1 Move to the start of your document. Pull down the View menu and click Header and Footer.

2 Insert the relevant text

5 Click Close to return to normal document editing

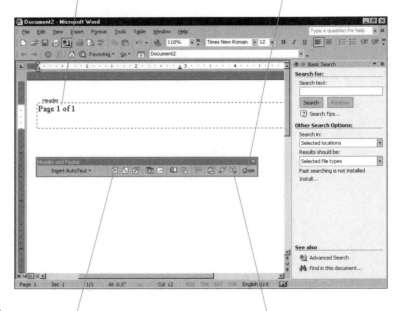

Header/footer text can be formatted in the normal way. For instance, you can apply a new font and/or type size...

You can have Word 2002 insert a special code which automatically inserts the page number – see step 3.

3 Click here to insert a page number code

4 Optional – click here to move to the header on the next page

Inserting bookmarks

In computer terms, a bookmark is a marker inserted to enable you to find a given location in a document easily and quickly.

Creating a bookmark

Place the insertion point where you want the bookmark inserted. Pull down the Insert menu and click Bookmark. Now do the following:

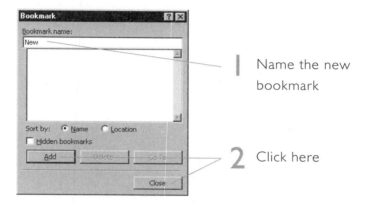

| Name the new bookmark

2 Click here

Jumping to a bookmark

Pull down the Insert menu and click Bookmark. Now do the following:

To delete a bookmark, carry out step 1 on the immediate right. Click this button:

Delete

then follow step 3.

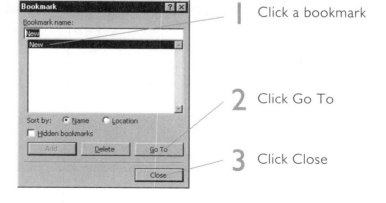

| Click a bookmark

2 Click Go To

3 Click Close

Inserting hyperlinks

You can insert hyperlinks into Word documents. Hyperlinks are text or graphics linked to:

To amend a bookmark hyperlink, place the insertion point within it (for text hyperlinks) or select the picture (for picture hyperlinks). Follow steps 1-2. In steps 3-4, make the necessary changes. Finally, carry out step 5.

- another location (e.g. a pre-inserted bookmark) in the same document, or;

- a document on the World Wide Web or an Intranet

Creating a hyperlink to a bookmark

Select the text or graphic you want to be the source of the link. Pull down the Insert menu and do the following:

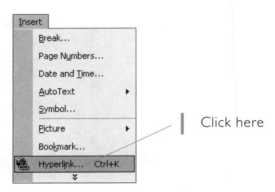

Click here

To delete a bookmark hyperlink, place the insertion point within it (for text hyperlinks) or select the picture (for picture hyperlinks). Follow steps 1-2. Now click Remove Link.

2 Click here

4 Insert the text you want to display for the hyperlink

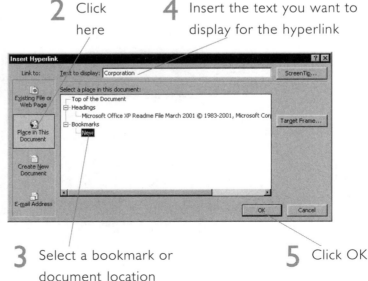

3 Select a bookmark or document location

5 Click OK

To activate a hyperlink, move the mouse pointer over it. Hold down Ctrl and click once.

To activate a hyperlink to a World Wide Web document, first ensure your Internet connection is live.

Creating a hyperlink to a Web or Intranet HTML file

Select the text or graphic you want to be the source of the link. Pull down the Insert menu and do the following:

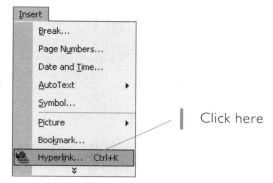

Click here

To create a hyperlink to a new document, click Create New Document. In the dialog, enter the new document name/address, decide whether you want to edit it now or later and name the hyperlink. Click OK.

To create a hyperlink to an email address, click E-Mail Address. In the dialog, enter the email address and name the hyperlink. Click OK.

2 Click here

4 Insert the text you want to display for the hyperlink

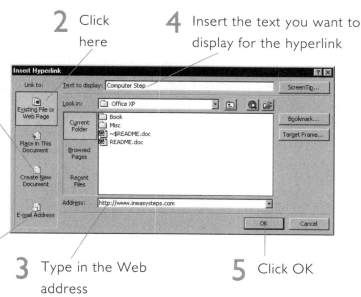

3 Type in the Web address

5 Click OK

Undo and redo

Re the tip below – remember, if you've used the Redo button before, Word 2002 may have promoted it to the main body of the Standard toolbar.

Word lets you reverse – 'undo' – just about any editing operation. If, subsequently, you decide that you do want to proceed with an operation that you've reversed, you can 'redo' it.

You can even undo or redo a series of operations in one go.

You can undo and redo actions in the following ways (in descending order of complexity):

- via the keyboard

- from within the Edit menu

To redo an action, click on the right of the toolbar. In the flyout, do the following:

- from within the Standard toolbar

Using the keyboard
Simply press Ctrl+Z to undo an action, or Ctrl+Y to reinstate it.

Using the Edit menu
Pull down the Edit menu and click Undo... or Redo... as appropriate (the ellipses denote the precise nature of the action to be reversed or reinstated).

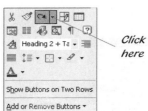
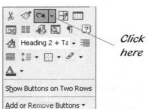

Click here

In the list, select a redo action (but the HOT TIP below also applies).

Using the Standard toolbar
Carry out the following action to undo an action (see the DON'T FORGET tip for how to reinstate it):

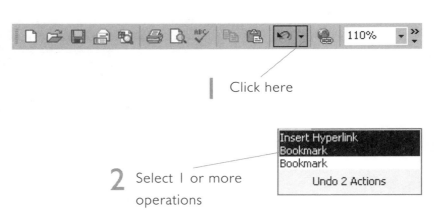

Click here

Re step 2 – if you select an early operation in the list (i.e. one near the bottom), all later operations are included.

2 Select 1 or more operations

Inspecting text styles

You can only view the Style pane in Normal view.

Finding out which text style is in force

If you're in any doubt about which style is associated with text, you can arrange to view style names in a special pane to the left of text.

Pull down the Tools menu and click Options. Do the following:

Styles are named collections of associated formatting commands. The advantage of using styles is that you can apply more than one formatting enhancement to selected text in one go. Once a style is in place, you can change one or more elements of it and have Word 2002 apply the amendments automatically throughout the whole of the active document.

Generally, new documents you create in Word 2002 are based on the NORMAL.DOT template and provide access to a variety of pre-defined styles, including some specialised ones aimed at the Web.

1 Activate the View tab

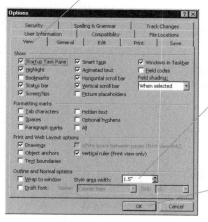

2 Type in a pane size – e.g. 1.2" (to hide the Style Pane, enter 0")

3 Click here

4 To view the Style pane, pull down the View menu and click Normal:

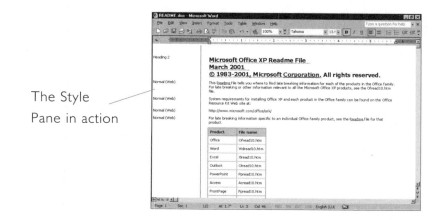

The Style Pane in action

Creating a text style

By default, Word 2002 applies the following names to new styles: 'Style 1', 'Style 2' etc.

The easiest way to create a style is to:

A.   apply the appropriate formatting enhancements to specific text and then select it

B.   tell Word to save this formatting as a style

First, carry out A. above. Then pull down the Format menu and click Styles and Formatting. Now do the following:

| Click New Style

If you want any manual amendments you make to the new style to be automatically incorporated in the style (but only in the active document), tick Automatically update.

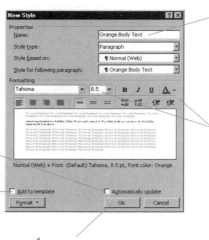

2 Name the style

3 Optional – adjust the style formatting (e.g. to increase or decrease the type size, enter a new one)

Tick Add to template if you don't just want your new style to be available for the active document.

4 Click here

Searching for synonyms

Word 2002's Thesaurus may not be installed (Install on Demand in action).
If it isn't, follow the on-screen instructions after clicking Language, Thesaurus in the Tools menu.

Word 2002 lets you search for synonyms while you're editing the active document. You do this by calling up Word's resident Thesaurus. The Thesaurus categorises words into meanings; each meaning is allocated various synonyms from which you can choose.

As a bonus, the Thesaurus also supplies antonyms. For example, if you look up 'good' in the Thesaurus (as below), Word lists 'poor' as an antonym.

Using the thesaurus

First, select the word for which you require a synonym or antonym (or simply position the insertion point within it). Pull down the Tools menu and click Language, Thesaurus. Now do the following:

If you've set up Office XP to work with specific additional languages (see page 25), Word automatically:

- *detects the language being used, and;*
- *applies the correct proofing tools (spell- and grammar-check, AutoCorrect etc.)*

The selected word appears here

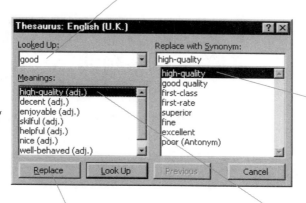

2 Click a replacement synonym or antonym

3 Click here to substitute the synonym or antonym for the selected word

Click the appropriate meaning

Translating text

You can also make use of free Web-based translation services – see below.

As long as the relevant dictionary has been installed, you can translate text from within Word.

Translating in Word

1   Pull down the Tools menu and select Languages, Translate

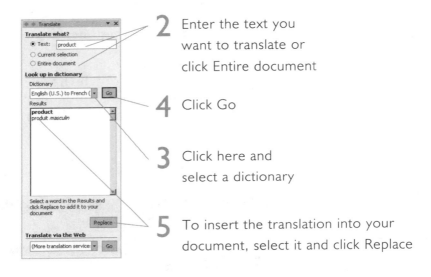

2   Enter the text you want to translate or click Entire document

4   Click Go

3   Click here and select a dictionary

5   To insert the translation into your document, select it and click Replace

Translating via the Web

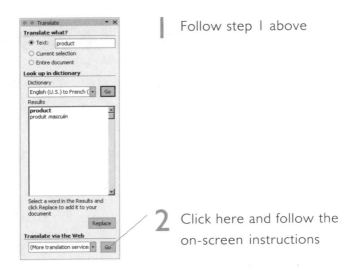

1   Follow step 1 above

2   Click here and follow the on-screen instructions

Working with pictures

You can have Word 2002 insert pictures automatically, by using its AutoCorrect feature.

To set up a picture as an AutoCorrect entry, select it. Pull down the Tools menu and click AutoCorrect. In the Replace field, insert the word/phrase you want the picture to replace. Select Formatted text. Click Add, followed by OK.

Word 2002 lets you add colour and greyscale pictures to the active document. Pictures – also called graphics – include:

- drawings produced in other programs

- clip art

- scanned photographs

Pictures are stored in various third-party formats. These formats are organised into two basic types:

Bitmap images

Bitmaps consist of pixels (dots) arranged in such a way that they form a graphic image. Because of the very nature of bitmaps, the question of 'resolution' – the sharpness of an image expressed in dpi (dots per inch) – is very important. Bitmaps look best if they're displayed at their correct resolution. Word 2002 can manipulate a wide variety of third-party bitmap graphics formats. These include: PCX, TIF, TGA and GIF.

To insert a picture stored as an AutoCorrect entry, do the following:

1. *type in the verbal trigger you set in the HOT TIP above*

2. *press Space (or any other punctuation). Alternatively, press Enter or Return*

Vector images

You can also insert vector graphics files into Word 2002 documents. Vector images consist of and are defined by algebraic equations. They're less complex than bitmaps and contain less detail. Vector files can also include bitmap information.

Irrespective of the format type, Word 2002 can incorporate pictures with the help of special 'filters'. These are special mini-programs whose job it is to translate third-party formats into a form which Word can use.

You can have Word compress images within documents (making them smaller). In the Picture toolbar, click this button:

Complete the Compress Pictures dialog.

Brief notes on picture formats

Two further much-used graphical/ image formats are:

- *Windows Bitmap. A popular bitmap format. File suffix: BMP*
- *Windows Metafile. A frequently used vector format. Can be used for information exchange between just about all Windows programs. File suffix: WMF*

To crop an image (i.e. to trim its edges so it fits a smaller space or to remove unwanted parts), click this button in the Picture toolbar (View, Toolbars, Picture):

Now select the picture you want to crop. Move the mouse pointer over one of the available handles. Drag the handle inwards.

Graphics formats Word 2002 will accept include the following (the column on the left shows the relevant file suffix):

CGM   Computer Graphics Metafile. A vector format frequently used in the past, especially as a medium for clip-art transmission. Less often used nowadays.

EPS   Encapsulated PostScript. Perhaps the most widely used PostScript format. PostScript combines vector *and* bitmap data very successfully. Incorporates a low-resolution bitmap 'header' for preview purposes.

GIF   Graphics Interchange Format. Developed for the on-line transmission of graphics data over the Internet. Just about any Windows program – and a lot more besides – will read GIF. Disadvantage: it can't handle more than 256 colours. Compression is supported.

PCD   (Kodak) PhotoCD. Used primarily to store photographs on CD.

PCX   An old stand-by. Originated with PC Paintbrush, a paint program. Used for years to transfer graphics data between Windows applications.

TGA   Targa. A high-end format, and also a bridge with so-called low-end computers (e.g. Amiga and Atari). Often used in PC and Mac paint and ray-tracing programs because of its high-resolution colour fidelity.

TIFF   Tagged Image File Format. Suffix: TIF. If anything, even more widely used than PCX, across a whole range of platforms and applications.

Inserting pictures

You can use Click and Type to insert pictures in blank page areas.

Inserting pictures via the Insert Clip Art Task Pane

First, position the insertion point at the location within the active document where you want to insert the picture. Pull down the Insert menu and click Picture, Clip Art. Do the following:

| Enter one or more keywords

Clips have associated keywords. You can use these to locate clips.

3 Click Search

You can add new clips to collections (or add new keywords to existing clips) in the Clip Organizer.
Click here to launch it:

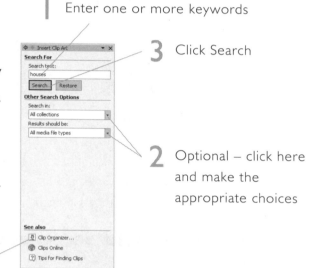

2 Optional – click here and make the appropriate choices

To conduct another search, click the Modify button then repeat steps 1-3.

4 Click an icon to insert the clip

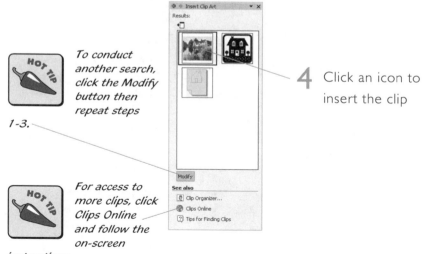

For access to more clips, click Clips Online and follow the on-screen instructions.

You can use Click and Type to insert pictures in blank page areas.

Inserting pictures – the dialog route

First, position the insertion point at the location within the active document where you want to insert the picture. Pull down the Insert menu and do the following:

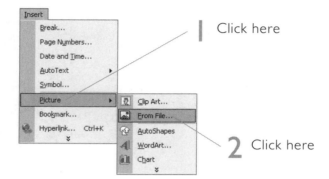

| Click here

2 Click here

4 Click here. In the drop-down list, click the drive/folder that hosts the picture

Word 2002 provides a preview of what the picture will look like when it's been imported – see the Preview box on the right of the dialog.

If this isn't visible, click the following toolbar icon repeatedly until it is:

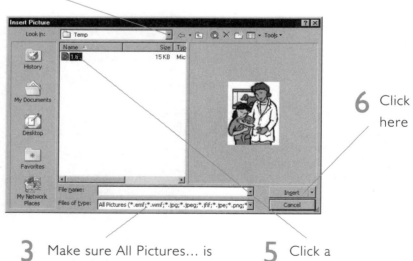

6 Click here

3 Make sure All Pictures... is showing. If it isn't, click the arrow and select it from the drop-down list

5 Click a picture file

Editing pictures

To move a picture on the page, select it. Then move the mouse pointer over the picture and drag it to a new location.

To rescale a picture, first select it. Then move the mouse pointer over:

- *one of the corner handles, if you want to rescale the image proportionately, or;*
- *one of the handles in the middle of the sides, if you want to warp it*

In either case, the mouse pointer changes to a double-headed arrow. Drag outwards to increase the image size or inwards to decrease it.

To control how text aligns around a picture, select it. Pull down the Format menu and click Picture. In the dialog, activate the Layout tab. Select a wrap option e.g.:

where text aligns around the top and bottom of the image, but not the sides. Finally, click OK.

Once you've inserted pictures into a Word 2002 document, you can amend them in a variety of ways. For instance, you can:

- rescale them

- apply a border

- crop them

- move them

To carry out any of these operations, you have to select the relevant picture first. To do this, simply position the mouse pointer over the image and left-click once. Word surrounds the image with eight handles. These are positioned at the four corners, and midway on each side. The illustration below demonstrates these:

Handles

Handles

Inserting watermarks

To preview watermarks, use Print Layout view or Print Preview.

You can add watermarks (graphics or text printed above or below document text) to Word pages.

Adding a watermark

In Web Layout view, you can insert backgrounds. These are designed to enhance Web viewing (when you export the file to HTML) but don't print.

Pull down the Format menu and click Background, Fill Effects. Complete the Fill Effects dialog. For example, to add a gradient fill, select the Gradient tab. Choose how many colours you want to use, select the colours, specify the brightness/ transparency and finally select a shading style.

Click OK to apply the selected background.

1 Pull down the Format menu and click Background, Printed Watermark

2 To insert a picture watermark, tick Picture watermark then Select Picture. Use the dialog to find/select a picture. Also, select a scale and – optionally – Washout (makes it fainter)

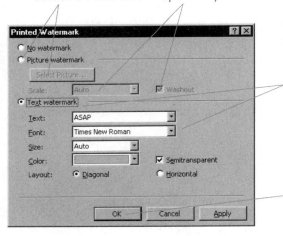

3 Alternatively, to insert a text watermark, select Text watermark and complete the text fields

4 Click here

To amend an existing watermark, follow step 1. Amend the settings in the Printed Watermark dialog then click OK.

To remove a watermark, follow step 1. Tick No watermark and click OK.

A text watermark, viewed in Print Preview

Bordering pictures

By default, Word 2002 does not apply a border to inserted pictures. However, you can apply a wide selection of borders if you want. You can specify:

- the style and/or thickness of the border
- the border colour
- whether the border is dashed

Applying a border

First, select the picture you want to border. Then pull down the Format menu and click Borders and Shading. Now carry out step 1 below. Perform 2–5, as appropriate. Finally, carry out step 6:

To specify a border width, do the following just before you carry out step 6:

Click here in the Width field; in the list, select a width

| Ensure the Borders tab is active

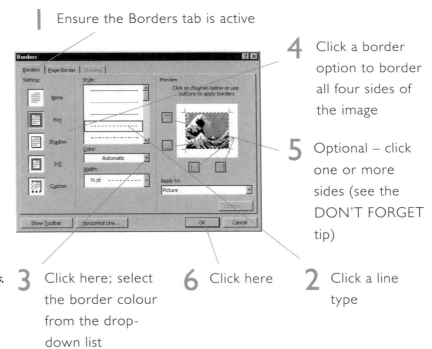

4 Click a border option to border all four sides of the image

5 Optional – click one or more sides (see the DON'T FORGET tip)

Use step 5 to deselect the top, bottom, left or right picture borders. (If you want to deselect more than one, repeat step 5 as often as necessary.)

3 Click here; select the border colour from the drop-down list

6 Click here

2 Click a line type

Page setup – an overview

You can control page layout to a great extent in Word 2002. You can specify:

- the top, bottom, left and/or right page margins

- the distance between the top page edge and the top edge of the header

- the distance between the bottom page edge and bottom edge of the footer

The illustration below shows these page components:

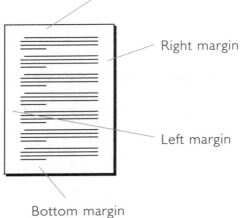

Top margin (including header)

Right margin

Left margin

Bottom margin
(including footer)

You can also specify:

- the page size (irrespective of margins and headers/footers)

- the page orientation ('landscape' or 'portrait')

If none of the supplied page sizes is suitable, you can even customise your own.

Specifying margins

Margin settings are the framework on which indents and tabs are based.

All documents have margins, because printing on the whole of a sheet is both unsightly and – in the case of many printers, since the mechanism has to grip the page – impossible. Documents need a certain amount of 'white space' (the unprinted portion of the page) to balance the areas which contain text and graphics. Without this, they can't be visually effective. As a result, it's important to set margins correctly.

Customising margins

First, position the insertion point at the location within the active document from which you want the new margin(s) to apply. Alternatively, select the relevant portion of your document. Then pull down the File menu and click Page Setup. Now carry out step 1 below. Then follow steps 2-3. Finally, carry out step 4.

To specify document orientation, click one of these:

Re step 3 – if you selected text before launching this dialog, click Selected text.

1 Ensure the Margins tab is active

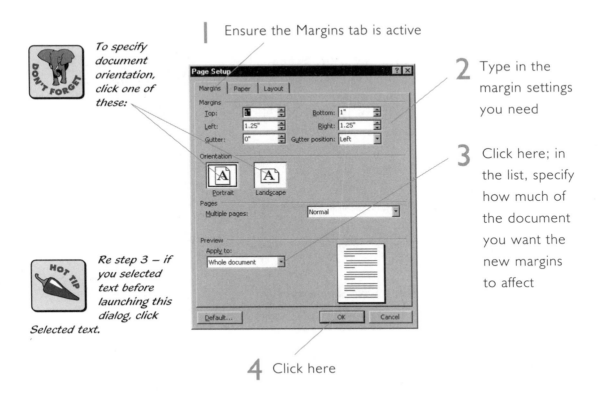

2 Type in the margin settings you need

3 Click here; in the list, specify how much of the document you want the new margins to affect

4 Click here

Specifying the page size

Whatever the page size, you can have both portrait and landscape pages in the same document.

(For how to specify page orientation, see the DON'T FORGET tip on page 87.)

Word 2002 comes with some 17 preset page sizes – for instance, A4, A5 and Letter. These are suitable for most purposes. However, you can also set up your own page definition if you need to.

There are two aspects to every page size: a vertical measurement, and a horizontal measurement. These can be varied according to orientation. There are two possible orientations:

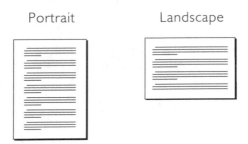

Portrait   Landscape

Setting the page size

First, position the insertion point at the location within the active document from which you want the new page size to apply. Then pull down the File menu and click Page Setup. Now do the following:

Re step 2 – to create your own page size, click Custom size. Then type in the correct measurements in the Width and Height fields.

Ensure the Paper tab is active

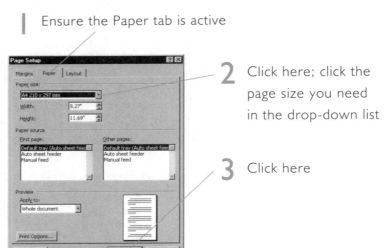

2   Click here; click the page size you need in the drop-down list

3   Click here

If you don't want your changes to affect the entire document, click the Apply to: field. In the list, select a more appropriate option (e.g. This point forward).

Using Print Preview

You can edit text directly from within Print Preview. With the magnifying cursor displaying, zoom in on the text you want to edit (see overleaf for how to do this). Click this button in the Print Preview toolbar:

Now click in the text and make the necessary changes.

Word 2002 provides a special view mode called Print Preview. This displays the active document exactly as it will look when printed. Use Print Preview as a final check just before you print your document.

You can customise the way Print Preview displays your document in various ways. For example, you can:

*   zoom in or out on the active page

*   specify how many pages display

*   hide almost everything on screen apart from the document

Launching Print Preview

Pull down the File menu and click Print Preview. This is the result:

We saw earlier that it's possible to hide superfluous screen components in Normal, Web Layout and Print Layout views. You can also do this in Print Preview mode. Word calls this Full Screen view. Full Screen view hides all screen components apart from the Print Preview and the Full Screen toolbar.

Click this button in the Print Preview toolbar:

To leave Full Screen view, press Esc.

Print Preview toolbar

Magnifying cursor

Press Esc to leave Print Preview

Zooming in or out in Print Preview

If you've just launched Print Preview, the Magnifier cursor will already be on-screen.

There are two ways in which you can change the display magnification in Print Preview mode.

Using the mouse

By default, the cursor in Print Preview is a magnifying glass – see the illustration on page 89 for what it looks like. You can use this to magnify *part* of the document.

If the cursor currently isn't a magnifying glass, do the following in the Print Preview toolbar:

In Print Preview mode, you can view as many as thirty-two (4 x 8) pages at the same time. Click this button:

Click here

Now position the Magnifier cursor over the portion of the active document that you want to expand. Left-click once.

Using the Zoom Control button

To choose from pre-defined Zoom sizes, do the following:

In the list, drag until you reach the correct view:

3 x 5 Pages

Click here

Using the Zoom Control button affects the whole of the active document.

2 Click a new Zoom option

Printer setup

Most Word 2002 documents need to be printed eventually. Before you can begin printing, however, you need to ensure that:

- the correct printer is selected (if you have more than one installed)

- the correct printer settings are in force

Word 2002 calls these collectively the 'printer setup'.

Irrespective of the printer selected, the settings vary in accordance with the job in hand. For example, most printer drivers (the software which 'drives' the printer) allow you to specify whether or not you want pictures printed. Additionally, they often allow you to specify the resolution or print quality of the output...

Selecting the printer and/or settings

At any time before you're ready to print a document, pull down the File menu and click Print. Now do the following:

Click here; select the printer you want from the list

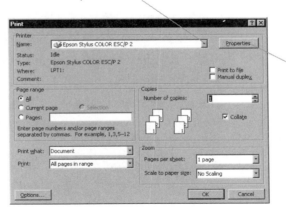

2 Click here to adjust printer settings (see your printer's manual for how to do this)

Now complete the remainder of the Print dialog, prior to printing your document.

Printing – an overview

Once the active document is how you want it (and you've customised the printer setup appropriately), you'll probably need to print it out. Word 2002 makes this process easy and straightforward. It lets you set a variety of options before you do so.

Alternatively, you can simply opt to print your document with the default options in force (Word 2002 provides a 'fast track' approach to this).

Available print options include:

You can preview HTML files or documents (in your default Web browser) directly from within Word. Pull down the File menu and click Web Page Preview.

- the number of copies you want printed

- whether you want the copies 'collated'. This is the process whereby Word 2002 prints one full copy at a time. For instance, if you're printing three copies of a 40-page document, Word prints pages 1-40 of the first document, followed by pages 1-40 of the second and pages 1-40 of the third

- which pages (or page ranges) you want printed

- whether you want to limit the print run to odd or even pages

- whether you want the print run restricted to text you selected before initiating printing

- whether you want the pages printed in reverse order (e.g. from the last page to the first)

- the quality of the eventual output (with many printers, Word 2002 allows you to print with minimal formatting for proofing purposes)

- whether you want to go on working in Word 2002 while the document prints (the default). Word 2002 calls this 'background printing'

You can 'mix and match' these, as appropriate.

Printing – the fast track approach

Since documents and printing needs vary dramatically, it's often necessary to customise print options before you begin printing. (See pages 94-95 for how to do this).

On the other hand, there are occasions when you'll merely want to print out your work:

- without having to invoke the Print dialog

- with the current settings applying

- with a single mouse click

One reason for doing this is proofing. Irrespective of how thoroughly you check documents on-screen, there will always be errors and deficiencies which, with the best will in the world, are difficult or impossible to pick up. By initiating printing with the minimum of delay, you can check your work that much more rapidly...

For this reason, Word 2002 provides a printing method which is quicker and easier to use.

Printing with the current print options

First, ensure your printer is ready and on-line. Make sure the Standard toolbar is visible. (If it isn't, pull down the View menu and click Toolbars, Standard). Now do the following:

You can also access fast-track printing from within Print Preview. Simply click this button:

Click here

in the Print Preview toolbar.

Word 2002 starts printing the active document immediately.

Customised printing

For more options, carry out the actions overleaf before you perform step 5 here.

If you need to set revised print options before printing, do the following.

Pull down the File menu and click Print. Now carry out steps 1-4, as appropriate. Finally, carry out step 5.

I | Click here to deselect collation

2 | Type in the number of copies

To print only odd or even pages, click the Print field. Click Odd Pages or Even Pages.

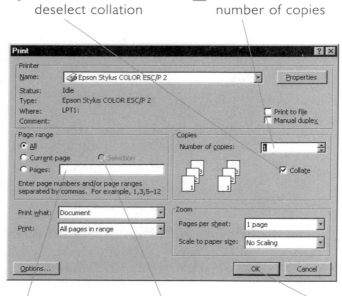

To print more than one page on a sheet, click Pages per sheet. Select a number in the list.

Re step 3 – separate non-adjacent pages with commas but no spaces – e.g. to print pages 5, 12, 16 and 19 type in:

5,12,16,19

Enter contiguous pages with dashes – e.g. to print pages 12 to 23 inclusive, type in:

12-23

3 | Type in the relevant page range (see tip opposite)

4 | Click here if you selected text before launching this dialog and this is all you want to print

5 | Click here

Word starts printing the active document.

Other print options are accessible from within a special dialog. This is launched from within the Print dialog.

First, pull down the File menu and click Print. Then do the following:

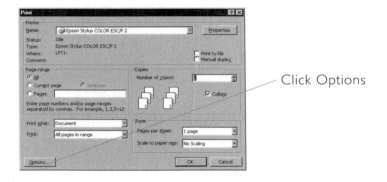

Click Options

Re step 2 – if you want to speed up printing, deselect background printing. (But note that if you do this, you won't be able to continue working until printing is complete.)

Perform steps 1-3 below, as appropriate. Then follow step 4.

1 Ensure this is selected to print with minimal formatting

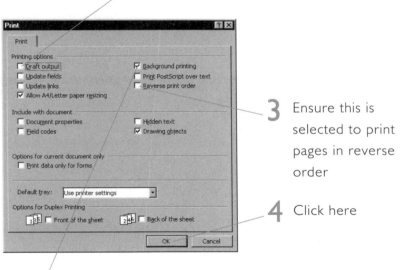

Step 4 returns you to the Print dialog. Now follow step 5 on the facing page to initiate printing.

3 Ensure this is selected to print pages in reverse order

4 Click here

2 Deselect this to turn off background printing

Handwriting text

To use handwriting recognition for the first time, you have to perform a custom install. Do this in the usual way but select Office Shared Features/Alternative User Input in Office's installer.

You can import handwritten notes made on a Handheld or Pocket PC into Word – see the device's documentation.

Re step 2 – click Write Anywhere to write directly on-screen, or On-Screen Standard Keyboard to use a virtual keyboard to enter text.

You can write with special devices (e.g. graphics tablets) or with the mouse.

By default, Word converts handwriting to text. However, you can have it entered as handwriting (which can be formatted in the normal way). Click this button in the Writing Pad:

You can handwrite text into a special writing pad and have Word convert it into standard text. You can also use a virtual keyboard to enter text.

1 If the Language Bar isn't visible or minimised on the Taskbar, go to Control Panel. Double-click Text Services. In the dialog, click Language Bar. Select Show the Language bar on the desktop. Click OK twice

2 Click Handwriting

3 Select Writing Pad

Language Bar

4 Handwrite text on the line in the Writing Pad (don't pause between letters but do leave a space after words) – Word enters the text as soon as it recognizes it

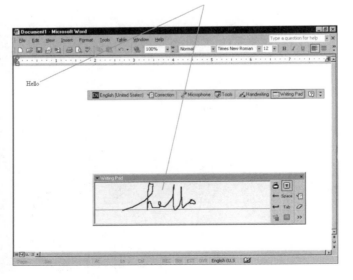

Excel 2002

Here, you'll become familiar with basic/advanced Excel use. You'll work with data, formulas/functions and error checking. You'll move around through worksheets and use the Watch Window to monitor cells. Then you'll format your worksheets for maximum effect and search for specific data. You'll use Smart Tags, insert pictures and convert your data into charts. Finally, you'll customise worksheet layout, preview your work and then print it.

Covers

Chapter Three

The Excel 2002 screen

Below is a detailed illustration of the Excel 2002 screen:

Title bar   Menu bar   Column letters

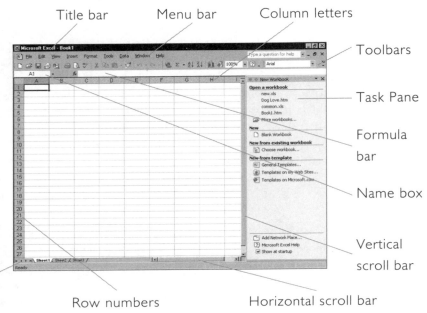

Toolbars

Task Pane

Formula bar

Name box

Vertical scroll bar

This is the worksheet Tab area. The screen components here are used to move through Excel documents.

Row numbers   Horizontal scroll bar

Some of these screen components can be hidden at will.

Specifying which screen components display

Pull down the Tools menu and click Options. Then:

Ensure the View tab is active

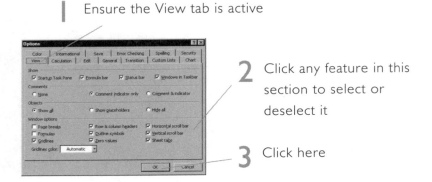

2 Click any feature in this section to select or deselect it

3 Click here

Entering data

When you start Excel 2002, you're presented with a new blank worksheet (spreadsheet):

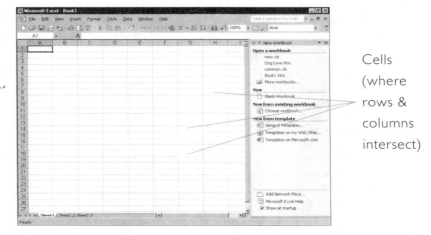

Cells (where rows & columns intersect)

This means that you can start entering data immediately.

In Excel, you can enter the following basic data types:

- values (i.e. numbers)

- text (e.g. headings and explanatory material)

- functions (e.g. Sine or Cosine)

- formulas (combinations of values, text and functions)

You enter data into 'cells'. Cells are formed where rows and columns intersect.

Beyond cells

Collections of rows/columns and cells are known in Excel as worksheets. Worksheets are organised into workbooks (by default, each workbook has 3 worksheets). Workbooks are the files that are stored on disk when you save your work in Excel.

When you enter values which are too big (physically) to fit in the holding cell, Excel 2002 may insert an error message.

To resolve this, widen the column (see the 'Amending row/column sizes' topic later). Or pull down the Format menu and click Column, Autofit Selection to have Excel automatically increase the column size to match the contents.

(See also page 113 for other error-checking procedures.)

Although you can enter data *directly* into a cell (by simply clicking in the cell and typing it in), there's another method you can use which is often easier. Excel provides a special screen component known as the Formula bar.

The illustration below shows the end of a blank worksheet. Some sample text has been inserted into cell IV65536 (note that the Name box tells you which cell is currently active).

Name box

Formula bar

Entering data via the Formula bar

Click the cell you want to insert data into. Then click the Formula bar. Type in the data. Then follow step 1 below. If you decide not to proceed with the operation, follow step 2 instead:

You can use a keyboard route to confirm operations in the Formula bar: simply press Enter.

1 Click here

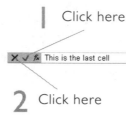

2 Click here

Modifying existing data

Re the tip below – the Redo button may not be in the main body of the toolbar. If so, click this button:

and access it in the fly-out.

You can amend the contents of a cell in two ways:

- via the Formula bar

- from within the cell

When you use either of these methods, Excel 2002 enters a special state known as Edit Mode.

Amending existing data using the Formula bar

Click the cell whose contents you want to change. Then click in the Formula bar. Make the appropriate revisions and/or additions. Then press Enter. Excel updates the relevant cell.

Amending existing data internally

Click the cell whose contents you want to change. Press F2. Make the appropriate revisions and/or additions *within the cell*. Then press Enter.

To redo an action, click the following button in the Standard toolbar:

In the list, select a redo action (but note that selecting an early operation – one near the bottom – will include all later operations).

The illustration below shows a section from a blank workbook:

A magnified view of cell G15, in Edit Mode (note the flashing insertion point)

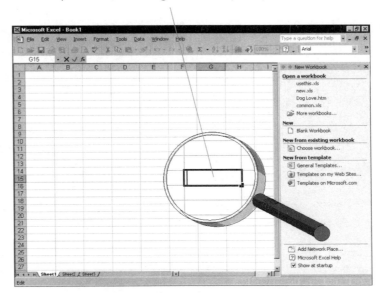

Working with cell ranges

When you're working with more than one cell, it's often convenient and useful to organise them in 'ranges'.

A range is a rectangular arrangement of cells. In the illustration below, cells A2, A3, A4, A5, A6, B2, B3, B4, B5 and B6 have been selected.

To undo one or more editing actions, you should carry out the following procedure in the Standard toolbar (or its fly-out):

—— Click here

Make your selection in the list but note that, if you select an early operation (i.e. one near the bottom), all later operations are included.

A selected cell range

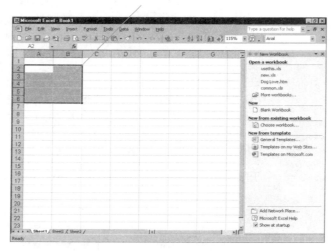

You can also use additional reference shortcuts (use the following as guides):

- All cells in row 15   15:15

- All cells in rows 8-20   8:20

- All cells in column A   A:A

- All cells in columns P-S   P:S

The above description of the relevant cells is very cumbersome. It's much more useful to use a form of shorthand. Excel 2002 (using the start and end cells as reference points) refers to these cells as:

A2:B6

You can extend this even more. Cell addresses can also incorporate a component which refers to the worksheet that contains the range. For example, to denote that the range A2:B6 is in a worksheet called Sheet8, you'd use:

Sheet8!A2:B6

Using Smart Tags

By default, Smart Tags are disabled. To turn them on, choose Tools, AutoCorrect Options. Select the Smart Tags tab and tick Label data with smart tags. Click OK.

Excel 2002 recognises certain types of data and inserts a small purple triangle or blue box in the relevant cell. When you move the mouse pointer over the triangle/box an 'action button' appears which provides access to commands which would otherwise have to be accessed from menus/toolbars or other programs.

Two examples are:

The Paste Options button

Although most Smart Tags are turned off by default, the AutoCorrect, Paste, AutoFill and Trace Error functions still work.

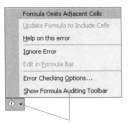

The Trace Error Smart Tag in action

| Here, we're pasting in '125' as a new value

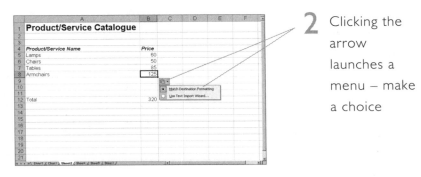

2 Clicking the arrow launches a menu – make a choice

Inserting stock symbols

You can search for and download more Smart Tags from the Web. Choose Tools, AutoCorrect Options. Select the Smart Tags tab and tick More Smart Tags. Follow the on-screen instructions.

| You can insert US stock symbols and have Excel provide Web-based information

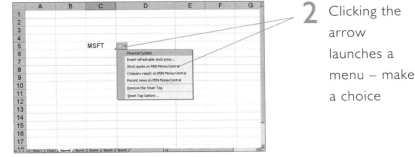

2 Clicking the arrow launches a menu – make a choice

Moving around in worksheets

Excel 2002 facilitates worksheet navigation. As you move the insertion point from cell to cell, the relevant row and column headers are highlighted:

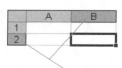

Illuminated headers

You can also use the following standard scroll bar techniques to navigate in worksheets:

- *to scroll quickly to another section of the active worksheet, drag the scroll box along the scroll bar until you reach it (hold down Shift to speed it up)*

- *to move one window to the right or left, click to the left or right of the scroll box in the horizontal scroll bar*

- *to move one window up or down, click above or below the scroll box in the vertical scroll bar*

- *to move up or down by one row, click the arrows in the vertical scroll bar*

- *to move left or right by one column, click the arrows in the horizontal scroll bar*

Using the keyboard
You can use the following techniques:

1. use the cursor keys to move one cell left, right, up or down

2. hold down Ctrl as you use 1. above; this jumps to the edge of the current section (e.g. if cell B11 is active and you hold down Ctrl as you press →, Excel jumps to IV11, the last cell in row 11)

3. press Home to jump to the first cell in the active row, or Ctrl+Home to move to A1

4. press Page Up or Page Down to move up or down by one screen

5. press Alt+Page Down to move one screen to the right, or Alt+Page Up to move one screen to the left

Using the Go To dialog
Excel 2002 provides a special dialog which you can use to specify precise cell destinations.

Pull down the Edit menu and click Go To. Now do the following:

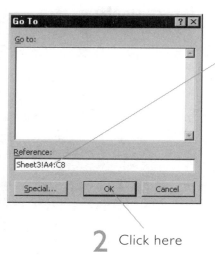

1 Type in the cell reference you want to move to – a cell's 'reference' identifies it in relation to its position in a worksheet, e.g. B11 or H23. You can also type in cell ranges here

2 Click here

Switching between worksheets

See the DON'T FORGET tip on page 98 if you're not sure how to find the *Tab area.*

Because workbooks have more than one worksheet, Excel provides two easy and convenient methods for moving between them.

Using the Tab area

You can use the Tab area (at the base of the Excel screen) to:

• jump to the first or last sheet

• jump to the next or previous sheet

• jump to a specific sheet

See the illustration below:

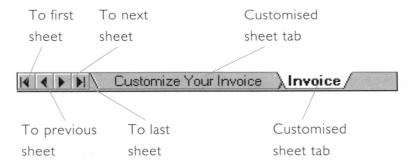

To first sheet   To next sheet   Customised sheet tab

To previous sheet   To last sheet   Customised sheet tab

When you click a worksheet tab, Excel 2002 emboldens the name and makes the tab background white.

To move to a specific sheet, simply click the relevant tab.

An example: in the illustration above, to jump to the 'Customize Your Invoice' worksheet, simply click the appropriate tab.

Using the keyboard

You can use keyboard shortcuts here:

Ctrl+Page Up   moves to the previous tab

Ctrl+Page Down   moves to the next tab

Viewing several worksheets

Excel 2002 also lets you view multiple worksheets simultaneously. This can be particularly useful when they have data in common. Viewing multiple worksheets is a two stage process:

A.   opening a new window

B.   selecting the additional worksheet

Opening a new window
Pull down the Window menu and do the following:

To switch between active windows, pull down the Window menu and click the relevant entry in the list at the bottom:

Click here

Selecting the additional worksheet
Excel now launches a new window showing an alternative view of the active worksheet. Do the following:

If you want to work with alternative views of the same worksheet – a useful technique in itself – simply omit step 2.

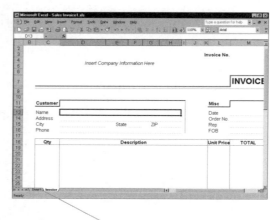

2   Click the relevant sheet tab

Rearranging worksheet windows

When you have multiple worksheet windows open at once, you can have Excel arrange them in specific patterns. This is a useful technique because it makes worksheets more visible and accessible. Options are:

Use standard Windows techniques to move, close and resize open windows.

Tiled — Windows are displayed side by side:

Horizontal — Windows are displayed in a tiled column, with horizontal subdivisions:

Vertical — Windows are displayed in a tiled row, with vertical subdivisions:

Cascade — Windows are overlaid (with a slight offset):

Rearranging windows

Pull down the Window menu and click Arrange. Then:

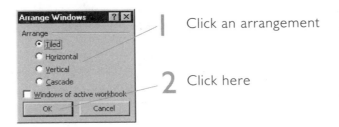

| Click an arrangement

2 Click here

Other operations on worksheets

You can use a keyboard shortcut to insert a worksheet.
Simply press Shift+F11.

To rearrange worksheets, first select 1 or more sheet tabs. With the mouse pointer still over the tab(s), drag them to their new location in the Tab area.

To move worksheets to another workbook, select 1 or more sheet tabs. Pull down the Edit menu and click Move or Copy Sheet. In the To book field, select a host workbook. Then click the worksheet in front of which you want the transferred sheet(s) to appear. Tick Create a copy if you want to copy rather than a move operation. Click OK.

We said earlier that, by default, each workbook has 3 worksheets. However, you can easily:

- add new worksheets

- delete existing worksheets

- move existing worksheets

Inserting a single worksheet

In the worksheet Tab area at the base of the screen, click the tab which represents the sheet in front of which you want the new worksheet inserted. Pull down the Insert menu and click Worksheet.

Inserting more than one worksheet

To add multiple worksheets, hold down one Shift key as you click the required number of sheet tabs (in other words, to add 6 new worksheets, shift-click 6 tabs). Then pull down the Insert menu and click Worksheet.

Deleting worksheets

In the worksheet Tab area, click a single worksheet tab (or shift-click multiple tabs to delete more than one worksheet at a time). Pull down the Edit menu and click Delete Sheet. Excel 2002 launches a special message. Do the following:

Click here to proceed with the deletion (the worksheet contents are automatically deleted, too)

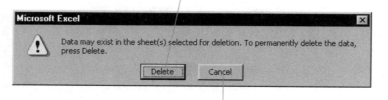

Or here to cancel it and return to your workbook

Using the Watch Window

The Watch Window is a great labour-saving device – it stops you having to continually switch between sheets or workbooks.

Excel provides a special toolbar called the Watch Window. As the name implies, you can use this to track cells (usually those containing formulas) while you're working on another part of the same worksheet, or another worksheet or workbook.

Launching the Watch Window

1 Right-click the cell you want to track

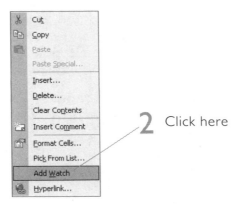

2 Click here

To remove a cell from the Watch Window, select its entry and click here:

3 The cell has been added to the Watch Window

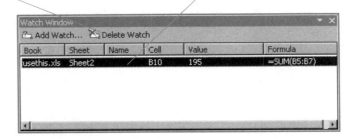

4 To call up the Watch Window when you don't want to add or remove cells, pull down the Tools menu and click Formula Auditing, Watch Window

Selection techniques

Before you can carry out any editing operations on cells in Excel 2002, you have to select them first. Selecting a single cell is very easy: you merely click in it. However, Excel provides a variety of selection techniques which you can use to select more than one cell.

Selecting adjacent cell ranges

The easiest way to do this is to use the mouse. Click in the first cell in the range; hold down the left mouse button and drag over the remaining cells. Release the mouse button.

You can use the keyboard, too. Select the first cell in the range. Hold down one Shift key as you use the relevant cursor key to extend the selection. Release the keys when the correct selection has been defined.

Selecting separate cell ranges

Excel lets you select more than one range at a time:

Selected ranges (cells, except the first, are see-through, so you can view changes to underlying data)

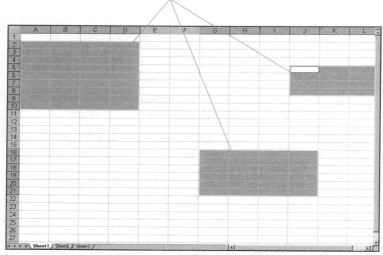

Click here

To select joint ranges, select the first in the normal way (you can only use the mouse method here). Then hold down Ctrl as you select subsequent ranges.

Formulas – an overview

Formulas are cell entries which define how other values relate to each other.

As a very simple example, consider the following:

The underlying formula – see below

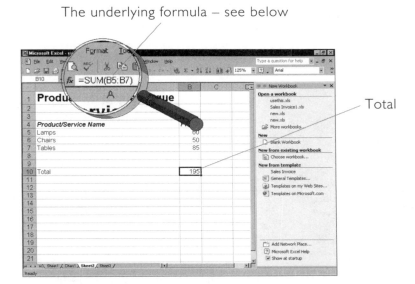

Total

Here, a cell has been defined which returns the total of cells B5:B7. Obviously, in this instance you could insert the total easily enough yourself because the individual values are so small, and because we're only dealing with a small number of cells. But what happens if the cell values are larger and/or more numerous, or – more to the point – if they're liable to change frequently?

The answer is to insert a formula which carries out the necessary calculation automatically.

If you look at the Formula bar in the illustration, you'll see the formula which does this:

=SUM(B5:B7)

Many Excel formulas are much more complex than this, but the principles remain the same.

Inserting a formula

Arguments (e.g. cell references) relating to functions are always contained in brackets.

All formulas in Excel 2002 begin with an equals sign. This is usually followed by a permutation of the following:

- an operand (cell reference, e.g. B4)

- a function (e.g. the summation function, SUM)

- an arithmetical operator (+, –, / and *)

- comparison operators (<, >, <=, >= and =)

Excel supports a very wide range of functions organised into numerous categories. For more information on how to insert functions, see page 114.

The mathematical operators are (in the order in which they appear in the list): *plus*, *minus*, *divide* and *multiply*.

To enter the same formula into a cell range, select the range, type the formula and then press Ctrl+Enter.

The comparison operators are (in the order in which they appear in the list): *less than*, *greater than*, *less than or equal to*, *greater than or equal to* and *equals*.

There are two ways to enter formulas:

Entering a formula directly into the cell

Click the cell in which you want to insert a formula. Then type = followed by your formula. When you've finished, press Enter.

Entering a formula into the Formula bar

This is usually the most convenient method.

Click the cell in which you want to insert a formula. Then click in the Formula bar. Type = followed by your formula. When you've finished, press Enter or do the following:

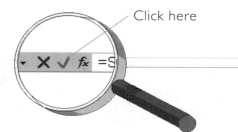

Click here

Using the Formula Evaluator

When formulas become complex (as they frequently do), it can be difficult to see how Excel arrives at the eventual result. However, you can now use a feature called Formula Evaluator to step through each calculation.

Using Formula Evaluator

| Select the cell which contains the formula. Pull down the Tools menu and click Formula Auditing, Evaluate Formula

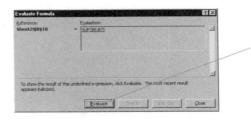

2 Click Evaluate – repeat as often as required

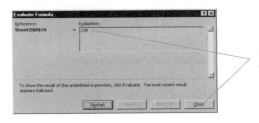

3 Each step is shown here – click Close when you've finished

Using the Formula Auditing toolbar

Precedents are cells referred to by formulas in other cells. Dependents are cells with formulas which refer to other cells. Activating the relevant buttons in the toolbar inserts lines making precedents and dependents visible, useful for error-checking.

| Choose View, Toolbars, Formula Auditing Toolbar

Check sheet for errors

Show/hide dependents

Launch Formula Evaluator

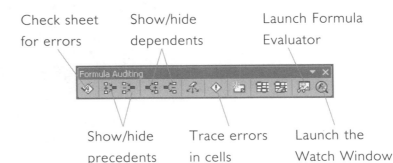

Show/hide precedents

Trace errors in cells

Launch the Watch Window

Inserting a function

Functions are pre-defined tools which accomplish specific tasks. These tasks are often calculations; occasionally, however, they're more generalised (e.g. some functions simply return dates and/or times). In effect, functions replace one or more formulas.

Functions can only be used in formulas.

- *Financial*
- *Date & Time*
- *Statistical*
- *Text*

Inserting a function

1 At the relevant juncture while inserting a formula, refer to the Formula bar and click this button: fx

If you know the function you want and it's fairly simple, you can enter it directly into a cell (preceded by =). When you do this, Excel often launches a ToolTip e.g.:

2 Type in a brief description of the function you want and click here

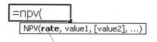

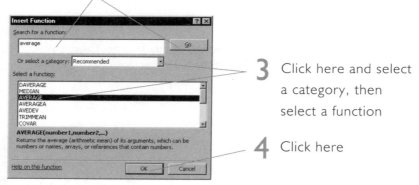

A helpful ToolTip – clicking an argument or function often launches HELP

3 Click here and select a category, then select a function

4 Click here

5 Enter the function arguments

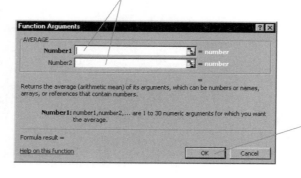

6 Click here

Amending row/column sizes

Sooner or later, you'll find it necessary to resize rows or columns. This necessity arises when there is too much data in cells to display adequately. You can enlarge or shrink single or multiple rows/columns.

Changing row height

To change one row's height, click the row heading. If you want to change multiple rows, hold down Ctrl and click the appropriate extra headings. Then place the mouse pointer (it changes to a cross) just under the row heading(s). Hold down the left mouse button and drag up or down to decrease or increase the row(s) respectively. Release the mouse button to confirm the operation.

Excel has a useful 'Best Fit' feature. When the mouse pointer has changed to:

double-click to have the row(s) or column(s) adjust themselves automatically to their contents.

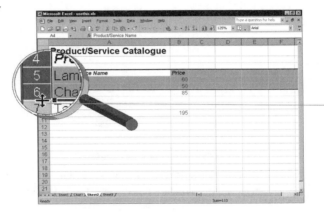

A magnified view of the transformed pointer – here, we're amending rows 4, 5 and 6 jointly

Changing column width

To change one column's width, click the column heading. If you want to change multiple columns, hold down Ctrl and click the appropriate extra headings. Then place the mouse pointer (it changes to a cross) just to the right of the column heading(s). Hold down the left mouse button and drag right or left to widen or narrow the column(s) respectively. Release the mouse button to confirm the operation.

Inserting cells, rows or columns

If you select cells in more than one row or column, Excel 2002 inserts the equivalent number of new rows or columns.

You can insert additional cells, rows or columns into worksheets.

Inserting a new row or column

First, select one or more cells within the row(s) or column(s) where you want to carry out the insert operation. Now pull down the Insert menu and click Rows or Columns, as appropriate. Excel 2002 inserts the new row(s) or column(s) immediately.

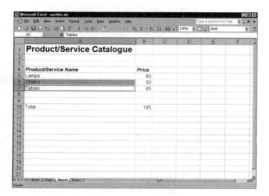

Here, one new column or two new rows are being added

Inserting a new cell range

Select the range where you want to insert the new cells. Pull down the Insert menu and click Cells. Now carry out step 1 or step 2 below. Finally, follow step 3.

1 Click here to have Excel make room for the new cells by moving the selected range *to the right*

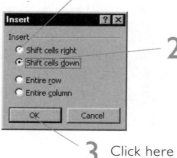

2 Click here to have Excel make room for the new cells by moving the selected range *down*

3 Click here

AutoFill

AutoFill extends formatting and formulas in lists.

Excel 2002 lets you insert data series automatically. This is a very useful and timesaving feature. Look at the illustration below:

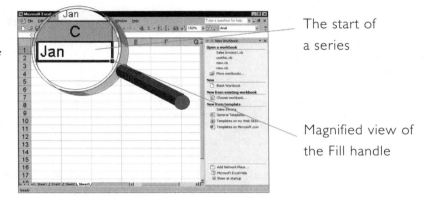

The start of a series

Magnified view of the Fill handle

Types of series you can use AutoFill to complete include:

- *1st Period, 2nd Period, 3rd Period etc.*
- *Mon, Tue, Wed etc.*
- *Quarter 1, Quarter 2, Quarter 3 etc.*
- *Week1, Week2, Week3 etc.*

If you wanted to insert month names in successive cells in column C, you could do so manually. But there's a much easier way. You can use Excel's AutoFill feature.

Using AutoFill to create a series

Type in the first element(s) of the series in consecutive cells. Select all the cells. Then position the mouse pointer over the Fill handle in the bottom right-hand corner of the last cell (the pointer changes to a crosshair). Drag the handle over the cells into which you want to extend the series (in the example above, over C2:C12). When you release the mouse button, Excel 2002 extrapolates the initial entry or entries into the appropriate series:

Data series don't need to contain every possibility. For instance, you could have:

- *1st Period, 3rd Period, 5th Period etc.*
- *Mon, Thu, Sun, Wed etc.*
- *Quarter 1, Quarter 4, Quarter 3, Quarter 2 etc.*
- *Week2, Week6, Week10, Week14 etc.*

The completed series

This is the AutoFill Smart Tag – move the pointer over it to produce an action button and menu:

	B	C
1		Jan
2		Feb
3		Mar
4		Apr
5		May
6		Jun
7		Jul
8		Aug
9		Sep
10		Oct
11		Nov
12		Dec
13		

- Copy Cells
- Fill Series
- Fill Formatting Only
- Fill Without Formatting
- Fill Months

Changing number formats

Excel 2002 lets you insert and work with Euros. Do the following.

To insert the Euro symbol, hold down Alt and press the following on the Numerical keypad to the right of your keyboard:

0128

Finally, release the Alt key.

Note that the following fonts currently support the Euro symbol:

- *Courier*
- *Tahoma*
- *Times*
- *Arial*

If a cell has had the Date number format applied, dates appear by default in a specific format. For example, '12th March 2002' is shown as:

12/03/2002

However, you can easily change this. Simply specify a new format (e.g. '14.3.01') in step 3.

Re step 3 – the options you can choose from vary according to the category chosen. Complete them as necessary.

Excel 2002 lets you apply formatting enhancements to cells and their contents. You can:

- specify a number format

- customise the font, type size and style of contents

- specify cell alignment

- border and/or shade cells

Specifying a number format

You can customise the way cell contents (e.g. numbers and dates/times) display in Excel. For example, you can specify at what point numbers are rounded up. Available formats are organised under several general categories. These include: Number, Accounting and Fraction.

Select the cells whose contents you want to customise. Pull down the Format menu and click Cells. Now do the following:

1 Ensure the Number tab is active

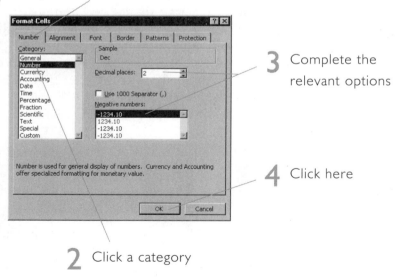

3 Complete the relevant options

4 Click here

2 Click a category

Changing fonts and styles

Excel lets you carry out the following actions on cell contents (numbers and/or text). You can:

- apply a new font and/or type size

- apply a font style (for most fonts, you can choose from: Regular, Italic, Bold or Bold Italic)

- apply a colour

- apply a special effect: underlining, ~~strikethrough~~, superscript or subscript

Amending the appearance of cell contents

Select the cell(s) whose contents you want to reformat. Pull down the Format menu and click Cells. Carry out step 1 below. Now follow any of steps 2-5, as appropriate, or either or both of the HOT TIPS. Finally, carry out step 6.

To underline the specified contents, click the arrow to the right of the Underline box; select an underlining type in the list.

Ensure the Font tab is active

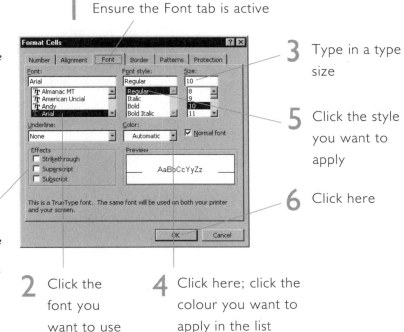

3 Type in a type size

5 Click the style you want to apply

6 Click here

To apply a special effect, click any of the options in the Effects section.

2 Click the font you want to use

4 Click here; click the colour you want to apply in the list

Cell alignment

By default, Excel aligns text to the left of cells, and numbers to the right. However, you can change this. Alignments come under two basic headings: horizontal and vertical.

You can also amend rotation (the direction of text flow within cells) by specifying a plus (anticlockwise) or minus (clockwise) angle. And you can apply text wrap – this forces any surplus text onto separate lines within the host cell (instead of overflowing into adjacent cells to the right).

	H	I	J
1	Here, text wrap is not in force		
2			
3			
4			
5	This text, however, *has* been wrapped		

— Text wrap in action

Customising cell alignment

Select the cell(s) whose contents you want to realign. Pull down the Format menu and click Cells. Carry out step 1 below. Follow steps 2-4, as appropriate, then finally step 5.

1   Ensure the Alignment tab is active

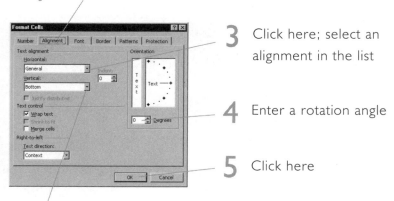

3   Click here; select an alignment in the list

4   Enter a rotation angle

5   Click here

2   Click here; select an alignment in the list

Bordering cells

Excel 2002 lets you define a border around:

- the perimeter of a selected cell range

- specific sides within a cell range

You can customise the border by choosing from a selection of pre-defined border styles. You can also add new line styles to specific sides, or colour the border.

Applying a cell border – the dialog route

First, select the cell range you want to border. Pull down the Format menu and click Cells. Now carry out step 1 below. Follow step 2 to apply an overall border. Carry out step 3 if you want to deactivate one or more border sides. Perform step 4 if you want to colour the border. Finally, carry out step 5:

If you want to customise the border style, click a line style here:

immediately after step 2. Omit step 3. Follow step 4 if you want to colour the new style. Now do the following in this part of the dialog:

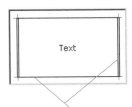

Click any of the 4 borders to apply the new style

Finally, carry out step 5.

1 Ensure the Border tab is active

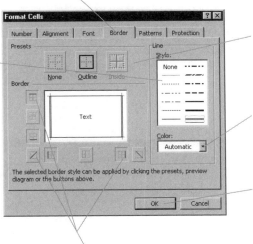

2 Click the relevant border style option

4 Optional – click here and select a colour in the list

5 Click here

3 Optional – click any border option in this section to deselect it

Applying a cell border – the Pencil route

You can handwrite text into Excel worksheets. For how to do this, follow the directions (as appropriate) on page 96.

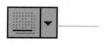

1 In the Formatting toolbar (or its fly-out), click here:

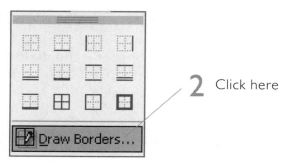

2 Click here

5 Ensure this is selected

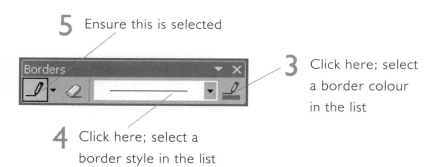

3 Click here; select a border colour in the list

4 Click here; select a border style in the list

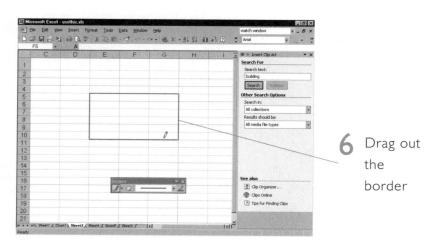

6 Drag out the border

Shading cells

Excel 2002 lets you apply the following to cells:

- a background colour

- a foreground pattern

- a foreground colour

Interesting effects can be achieved by using pattern and colour combinations with coloured backgrounds.

Applying a pattern or background

First, select the cell range you want to shade. Pull down the Format menu and click Cells. Now carry out step 1. Perform step 2 to apply a *background* colour, and/or 3-5 to apply a *foreground* pattern or a pattern/colour combination. Finally, follow step 6.

1 Ensure the Patterns tab is active

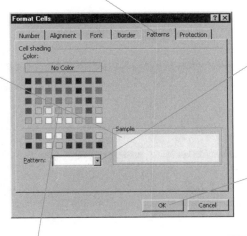

3 Click here to apply a foreground pattern or a pattern/colour combination

6 Click here

2 Click a colour here to apply it as a background

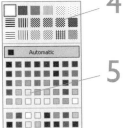

4 Click a pattern

5 Click a colour

AutoFormat

Excel 2002 provides a shortcut to the formatting of worksheet data: AutoFormat.

AutoFormat consists of 16 pre-defined formatting schemes. These incorporate specific excerpts from the font, number, alignment, border and shading options discussed earlier. You can apply any of these schemes (and their associated formatting) to selected cell ranges with just a few mouse clicks. You can even specify which scheme elements you *don't* wish to use.

AutoFormat works with most arrangements of worksheet data.

Using AutoFormat

First, select the cell range you want to apply an automatic format to. Pull down the Format menu and click AutoFormat. Now carry out step 1 below. Steps 2-3 are optional. Finally, follow step 4:

Select an AutoFormat

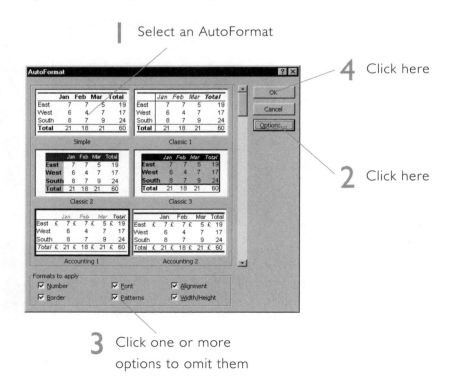

4 Click here

2 Click here

3 Click one or more options to omit them

The Format Painter

Excel 2002 provides a very useful tool which can save you a lot of time and effort: the Format Painter. You can use the Format Painter to copy the formatting attributes from cells you've previously formatted to other cells, in one operation.

Using the Format Painter

1 Apply the necessary formatting, if you haven't already done so. Then select the formatted cells

2 Click the Format Painter icon in the Standard toolbar (or its fly-out)

Re. step 1 – double-click the Format Painter icon if you want to apply the selected formatting more than once. Then repeat step 2 as often as necessary.
Press Esc when you've finished.

Pre-formatted text – see step 1

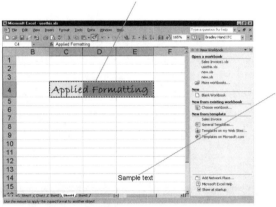

3 Select the cell(s) you want the formatting copied to

When you've finished using the Format Painter (or before, if you decide you don't want to proceed), press Esc.

The end result

Find operations

Excel 2002 lets you search for and jump to text or numbers (in short, any information) in your worksheets. This is a particularly useful feature when worksheets become large and complex.

You can organise your search by rows or by columns. You can also specify whether Excel looks in:

- cells that contain formulas

- cells that don't contain formulas

Additionally, you can insist that Excel only flag exact matches (i.e. if you searched for '11', Excel would not find '1111'), and you can also limit text searches to text which has the case you specified (e.g. searching for 'PRODUCT LIST' would not find 'Product List' or 'product list').

Searching for data

Place the mouse pointer at the location in the active worksheet from which you want the search to begin. Pull down the Edit menu and click Find. Now carry out step 1 below, then (optionally) 2. Finally, carry out step 3.

To search for data over more than one worksheet, select the relevant sheet tabs before launching the Find dialog.

If you want to restrict the search to specific cells, select a cell range before you launch the Find dialog.

Type in the data you want to find

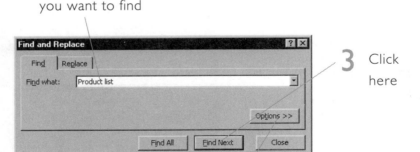

3 Click here

2 To specify the search direction, limit it to certain cell types or make it case-specific, click Options and complete the dialog which appears

Find-and-replace operations

When you search for data, you can also – if you want – have Excel 2002 replace it with something else.

Find-and-replace operations can be organised by rows or columns. However, unlike straight searches, you can't specify whether Excel looks in cells that contain formulas or not. As with straight searches, you can, however, limit find-and-replace operations to exact matches and also (in the case of text) to precise case matches.

Normally, find-and-replace operations only affect the host worksheet. If you want to carry out an operation over multiple worksheets, see the HOT TIP.

Running a find-and-replace operation

Place the mouse pointer at the location in the active worksheet from which you want the search to begin (or select a cell range if you want to restrict the find-and-replace operation to this). Pull down the Edit menu and click Replace. Now carry out steps 1-4 below. Finally, carry out step 5 as often as required, or perform step 6 once for a global substitution.

To replace data over more than one worksheet, select the relevant sheet tabs before launching the Replace dialog.

If, when you carry out step 5, Excel finds an instance of the search text you don't want replaced, simply repeat step 4 instead.

1 Type in the data you want to find

2 Type in replacement data

3 To set options (see step 2 on the facing page) click here

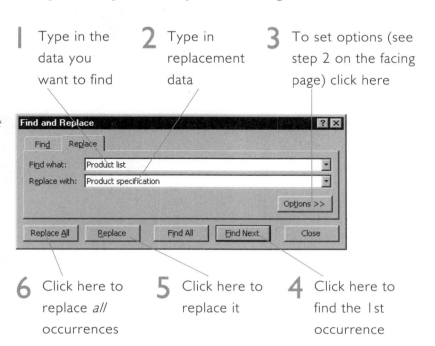

6 Click here to replace *all* occurrences

5 Click here to replace it

4 Click here to find the 1st occurrence

Charting – an overview

Excel 2002 has comprehensive charting capabilities. You can have it convert selected data into its visual equivalent. To do this, Excel offers a wide number of chart formats and sub-formats.

You can create a chart:

- as a picture within the parent worksheet

- as a separate chart sheet

Chart sheets have their own tabs in the Tab area; these operate just like worksheet tabs.

Excel uses a special Wizard – the Chart Wizard – to make the process of creating charts as easy and convenient as possible.

As here, you can add a picture to chart walls. See page 132.

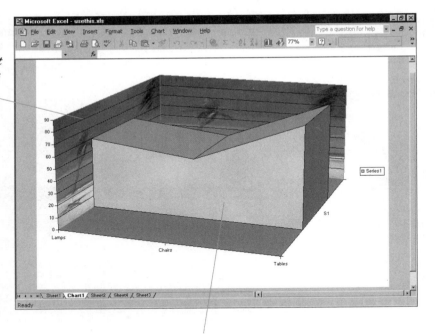

A 3-D Area chart

Creating a chart

First, select the cells you want converted into a chart. Pull down the Insert menu and click Chart. The first Chart Wizard dialog appears. Do the following:

Click a chart type

Click and hold here to have Excel preview the selected chart combination in the Chart sub-type field.

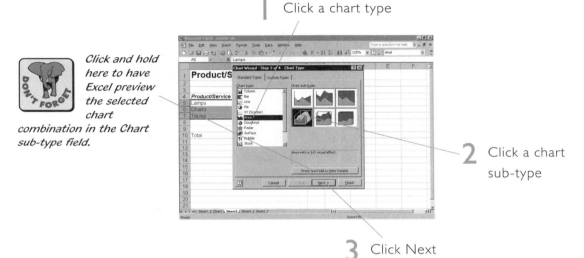

2 Click a chart sub-type

3 Click Next

Re step 4 – to hide the dialog temporarily while you select an alternative cell range, click the Collapse Dialog button:

There are three more dialogs to complete. Carry out the following steps:

When you've finished, do the following:

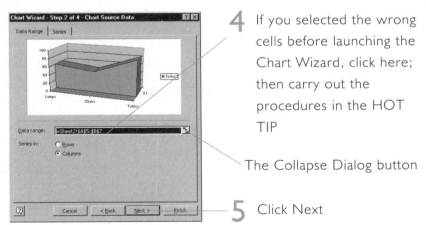

Click here

4 If you selected the wrong cells before launching the Chart Wizard, click here; then carry out the procedures in the HOT TIP

The Collapse Dialog button

5 Click Next

Click any of the additional tabs to set further chart options. For example, activate the Gridlines tab to specify how and where gridlines display. Or click Legend to determine where legends (text labels) display...

Excel 2002 now launches the third Chart Wizard dialog. Carry out the following additional steps:

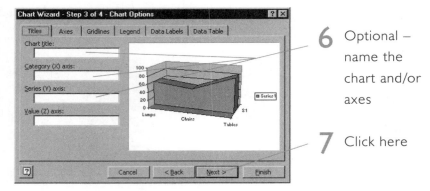

6 Optional – name the chart and/or axes

7 Click here

In the final dialog, you tell Excel whether you want the chart inserted into the current worksheet, or into a new chart sheet.

Carry out step 8 OR 9 below. Finally, perform step 10.

8 Click here to create a chart sheet

Re step 8 – if you don't want to use the default chart sheet name, you can type in a new one here.

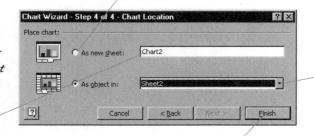

9 Click here; select an existing sheet in the list

10 Click here to generate the chart

Inserting pictures

Inserting pictures via the Insert Clip Art Task Pane

First, position the insertion point at the location within the active worksheet where you want to insert the picture. Pull down the Insert menu and click Picture, Clip Art. Do the following:

Enter one or more keywords

Clips have associated keywords. You can use these to locate clips.

3 Click Search

You can add new clips to collections (or add new keywords to existing clips) in the Clip Organizer.
Click here to launch it:

2 Optional – click here and make the appropriate choices

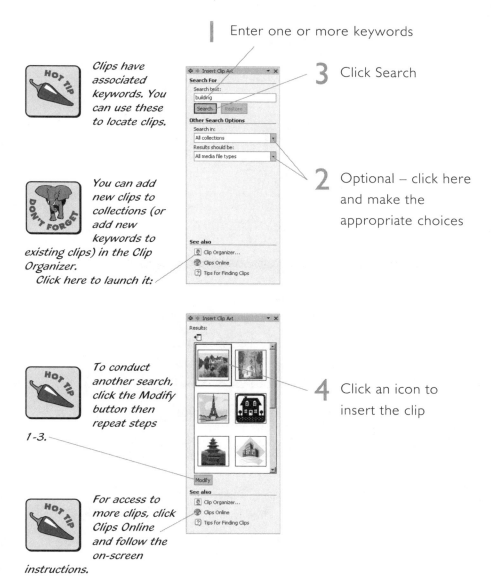

To conduct another search, click the Modify button then repeat steps 1-3.

4 Click an icon to insert the clip

For access to more clips, click Clips Online and follow the on-screen instructions.

Inserting pictures – the dialog route

First, position the insertion point at the location within the active worksheet where you want to insert the picture. Pull down the Insert menu and do the following:

Once inserted into a worksheet, pictures can be resized and moved in the normal way.

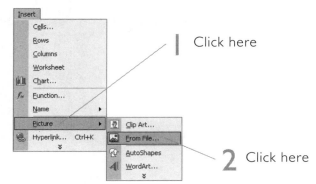

| Click here

2 Click here

You can insert pictures onto chart walls. First, select the chart wall then follow the procedures described here.

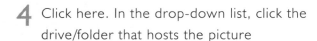

4 Click here. In the drop-down list, click the drive/folder that hosts the picture

6 Click here

Excel 2002 provides a preview of what the picture will look like when it's been imported – see the Preview box on the right of the dialog.

If this isn't visible, click the following toolbar icon repeatedly until it is:

3 Make sure All Pictures... is showing. If it isn't, click the arrow and select it from the drop-down list

5 Click a picture file

Page setup – an overview

Excel 2002 has a special view mode – Page Break Preview – which you can also use to ensure your worksheet prints correctly.

Pull down the View menu and click Page Break Preview. Do the following (the white area denotes cells which will print, the grey those which won't):

Drag page break margins to customise the printable area

(To leave Page Break Preview when you've finished with it, click Normal in the View menu.)

Making sure your worksheets print with the correct page setup can be a complex issue, for the simple reason that most worksheets become very extensive with the passage of time (so large, in fact, that in the normal course of things they won't fit onto a single page).

Page setup features you can customise include:

*   the paper size and orientation

*   scaling

*   the starting page number

*   the print quality

*   margins

*   header/footer information

*   page order

*   which worksheet components print

Margin settings you can amend are:

*   top

*   bottom

*   left

*   right

Additionally, you can set the distance between the top page edge and the top of the header, and the distance between the bottom page edge and the bottom edge of the footer.

When you save your active workbook, all Page Setup settings are saved with it.

Setting page options

Charts in separate chart sheets have unique page setup options – see page 138.

Excel 2002 comes with 17 pre-defined paper sizes which you can apply to your worksheets, in either portrait (top-to-bottom) or landscape (sideways on) orientation. This is one approach to effective printing. Another is scaling: you can print out your worksheets as they are, or you can have Excel shrink them so that they fit a given paper size (you can even automate this process). Additionally, you can set the print resolution and starting page number.

Using the Page tab in the Page Setup dialog

Pull down the File menu and click Page Setup. Now carry out step 1 below, followed by steps 2-6 as appropriate. Finally, carry out step 7:

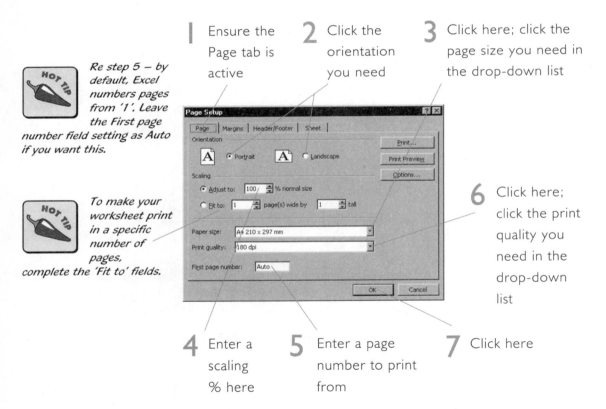

Re step 5 – by default, Excel numbers pages from '1'. Leave the First page number field setting as Auto if you want this.

To make your worksheet print in a specific number of pages, complete the 'Fit to' fields.

1 Ensure the Page tab is active

2 Click the orientation you need

3 Click here; click the page size you need in the drop-down list

6 Click here; click the print quality you need in the drop-down list

4 Enter a scaling % here

5 Enter a page number to print from

7 Click here

Setting margin options

Excel 2002 lets you set a variety of margin settings. The illustration below shows the main ones:

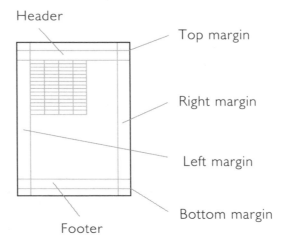

Header

Top margin

Right margin

Left margin

Bottom margin

Footer

Using the Margins tab in the Page Setup dialog

Pull down the File menu and click Page Setup. Now carry out step 1 below, followed by steps 2-3 as appropriate. Finally, carry out step 4:

1 Ensure the Margins tab is active

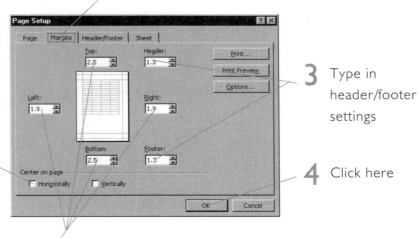

To specify how your worksheet aligns on the page, click either option here.

3 Type in header/footer settings

4 Click here

2 Type in the margin settings you need

Setting header/footer options

Excel 2002 provides a list of built-in header and footer settings. You can apply any of these to the active worksheet. These settings include:

- the worksheet title

- the workbook title

- the page number

- the user's name

- 'Confidential'

- the date

Using the Header/Footer tab in the Page Setup dialog

Pull down the File menu and click Page Setup. Now carry out step 1 below, followed by steps 2-3 as appropriate. Finally, carry out step 4:

1 | Ensure the Header/ Footer tab is active

2 Click here; select a header from the list

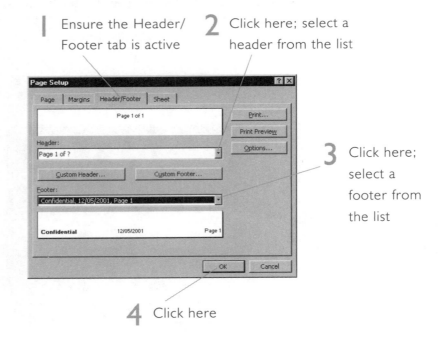

3 Click here; select a footer from the list

4 Click here

Setting sheet options

Excel 2002 lets you:

- define a printable area on-screen

- define a column or row title which will print on every page

- specify which worksheet components should print

- print with minimal formatting

- determine the print direction

Using the Sheet tab in the Page Setup dialog

Pull down the File menu and click Page Setup. Now carry out step 1 below, followed by steps 2-4 (and the tips) as appropriate. Finally, carry out step 5.

If you want to print a specific cell range (print area), type in the address here:

| Ensure the Sheet tab is active

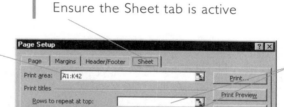

4 Type in the address of the row/column you want to use as a consistent title

Click Draft Quality for rapid printing with the minimum of formatting.

2 Click a direction option

3 Click a component to include or exclude it

5 Click here

Page setup for charts

Most page setup issues for charts in chart sheets are identical to those for worksheet data. The main difference, however, is that the Page Setup dialog has a Chart (rather than a Sheet) tab.

In the Chart tab, you can opt to have the chart

- printed at full size

- scaled to fit the page

- user-defined

You can also set the print quality.

Using the Chart tab in the Page Setup dialog
Click the relevant chart tab in the worksheet Tab area. Pull down the File menu and click Page Setup. Now carry out step 1 below, followed by steps 2-3 as appropriate. Finally, carry out step 4.

Re step 3 – clicking Custom ensures that, when you return to the chart sheet, the chart size can be adjusted with the mouse in the normal way. The chart then prints at whatever size you set.

Ensure the Chart tab is active

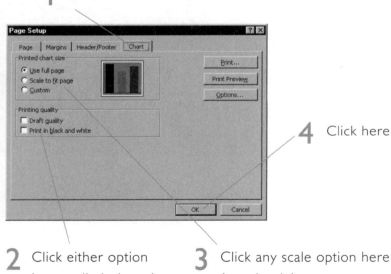

4 Click here

2 Click either option here to limit the print quality

3 Click any scale option here (see the tip)

Launching Print Preview

Print Preview displays data in greyscale (rather than colour).

Excel 2002 provides a special view mode called Print Preview. This displays the active worksheet as it will look when printed. Use Print Preview as a final check just before you begin printing.

You can perform the following actions from within Print Preview:

Excel's Print Preview mode only has the following Zoom settings:

- *Full Page*
- *High-Magnification*

- moving from page to page

- zooming in or out on the active page

- adjusting most Page Setup settings

- adjusting margins visually

Launching Print Preview

Pull down the File menu and click Print Preview. This is the result:

Special Print Preview toolbar

To leave Print Preview mode and return to your worksheet (or chart sheet), simply press Esc.

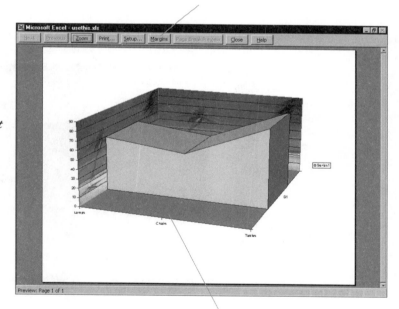

A preview of a chart sheet

Working with Print Preview

All of the operations you can perform in Print Preview mode can be accessed via the toolbar.

Click the Page Break Preview button to launch this view – see page 133 for how to use it.

Using the Print Preview toolbar

Do any of the following, as appropriate:

1 Click Next to jump to the next page

3 Click here to zoom in or out

6 Click here to launch the Page Setup dialog

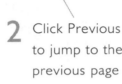

Re step 6 – see earlier topics for how to use the Page Setup dialog.

2 Click Previous to jump to the previous page

4 Click here to toggle margin markers on or off – then follow step 5

5 Drag any margin to reposition it

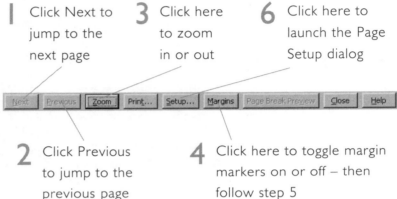

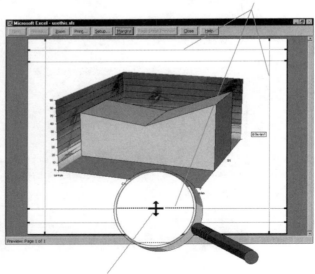

Magnified view of Move pointer

Printing worksheet data

Excel 2002 lets you specify:

- the number of copies you want printed

- whether you want the copies 'collated'. This is the process whereby Excel prints one full copy at a time. For instance, if you're printing three copies of a 10-page worksheet, Excel prints pages 1-10 of the first copy, followed by pages 1-10 of the second and pages 1-10 of the third.

- which pages (or page ranges) you want printed

- whether you want the print run restricted to cells you selected before initiating printing

You can 'mix and match' these, as appropriate.

To select and print more than one worksheet, hold down Shift as you click on multiple tabs in the worksheet Tab area.

Starting a print run

Open the workbook that contains the data you want to print. If you want to print an entire worksheet, click the relevant tab in the worksheet Tab area. If you need to print a specific cell range within a worksheet, select it. Then pull down the File menu and click Print. Do any of steps 1-5. Then carry out step 6 to begin printing.

To adjust your printer's internal settings before you initiate printing, click Properties: Then refer to your printer's manual.

1 Click here; select the printer you want from the list

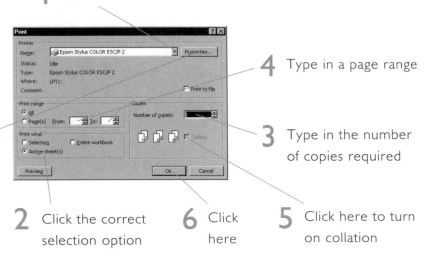

4 Type in a page range

3 Type in the number of copies required

2 Click the correct selection option

6 Click here

5 Click here to turn on collation

Printing – the fast track approach

There are occasions when you'll merely want to print out your work:

- without having to invoke the Print dialog

- with the current settings applying

- with a single mouse click

One reason for doing this is proofing. Irrespective of how thoroughly you check documents on-screen, there will always be errors and deficiencies which, with the best will in the world, are difficult or impossible to pick up. By initiating printing with the minimum of delay, you can check your work that much more rapidly...

For further coverage of essential Excel 2002 features, see 'Excel 2002', also in the 'in easy steps' series.

For this reason, Excel 2002 provides a printing method which is especially quick and easy to use.

Printing with the current print options

First, ensure your printer is ready and on-line. Make sure the Standard toolbar is visible. (If it isn't, pull down the View menu and click Toolbars, Standard). Now do the following:

Click here

Excel 2002 starts printing the active worksheet immediately, using the defaults listed above.

Using speech recognition

You can dictate text into any Office program (though to a slightly lesser extent in the case of Outlook) and have it turned into on-screen text. When errors occur, you can correct them with the mouse and keyboard (in the usual way) or by dictating the replacement. You can also launch menus, toolbar buttons and dialogs with dedicated voice commands.

Covers

Chapter Four

Preparing to use speech recognition

You can dictate text into any module. You can also make selections in menus, toolbars, dialogs and the Task Pane.

To use speech recognition, you need the following:

- a high-quality headset, preferably with USB (Universal Serial Bus) support and gain adjustment

- a minimum chip speed of 400 MHz (slower chips make dictation extremely laborious)

- a minimum of 128 Mb of RAM

- Windows 98 (or NT 4.0) or later

- Internet Explorer 5.0 (or later)

For more information on requirements, visit (no spaces or line breaks):

http://office.microsoft.com/ assistance/2002/articles/ oSpeechRequirements_aw. htm

Your use of speech recognition will benefit from repeated training. Click the Tools button on the Language Bar and select Training. Complete the wizard which launches.

Installing/running speech recognition

If you haven't installed speech recognition via a custom install, pull down the Word Tools menu and click Speech.

Preparing speech recognition

Before you can dictate into Office programs, you have to adjust your microphone and carry out a brief 'training' procedure to acclimatise Office to the sound of your voice:

1 In Word, PowerPoint or Outlook, pull down the Tools menu and click Speech. In Excel, choose Tools, Speech, Speech Recognition

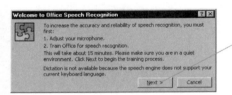

2 Click Next to begin the training process

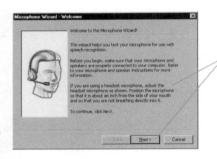

3 Adjust your microphone in line with the instructions then click Next

4 Read out the sentence shown then click Next. Complete the rest of the wizard

Dictating text

To start or end speech recognition in Word, PowerPoint or Outlook, choose Tools, Speech before step 1. In Excel, however, choose Tools, Speech, Speech Recognition.

Starting to dictate

1 If the microphone isn't already turned on, click here

To get the best out of speech recognition, you need to carry out the following:

2 The Language bar expands – click Dictation

- keep your environment as quiet as possible
- keep the microphone in the same position relative to your mouth
- run the training wizard as often as possible
- pronounce words clearly but don't pause between them or between individual letters – only pause at the end of your train of thought
- turn off the microphone when not in use (by repeating step 1)

3 Begin dictating. Initially, Office inserts a blue bar on the screen – the text appears as soon as it's recognised

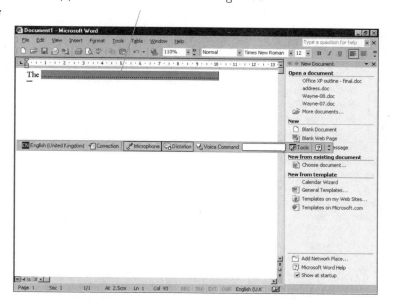

For the best results, use speech recognition in conjunction with mouse and keyboard use.

4 When you've finished, follow the procedure in the HOT TIP

Entering voice commands

You can switch to Voice Command by saying 'Voice Command', or dictation by saying 'Dictation'.

Follow step 1 on page 145

2 Click Voice Command

Commands you speak appear in the following Language bar field:

Task Pane

3 Issue the appropriate command e.g.:

- to launch the File menu say 'file' or 'file menu' (to select a menu entry say the name)

For more details of voice commands, see the HELP topic 'Getting started with speech recognition'.

- to open the Font dialog say 'font' (to select a typeface, say the name)
- to close a dialog say 'OK'
- to select a toolbar button, say the name
- to launch the Task Pane, say 'Task Pane'

Correcting errors

1 Replace wrong text with corrections in the usual way

If the Language Bar isn't visible or minimised on the Taskbar, go to Control Panel. Double-click Text Services. In the dialog, click Language Bar. Select Show the Language bar on the desktop. Click OK twice.

2 Or right-click the error. Choose a replacement in the menu or click More and select it from the list:

1	Force
2	cause
3	close
4	place
5	price
6	course
7	trust command
8	post command
9	forest command

Re step 4 – it's best to correct phrases rather than individual words.

3 Or select the error with your mouse. In Dictation mode, say 'spelling mode'. Now spell out the substitution e.g. n-o-w

4 Or select the error with your mouse. In Dictation mode, say the corrected version

PowerPoint 2002

Here, you'll produce your own professional-quality slide show. You'll automate the creation of a presentation and then customise it. You'll add/format text; work with slide views; insert pictures, diagrams, animations and hyperlinks; work with slide masters; and apply new design templates/ colour schemes. Finally, you'll print out your presentation and run it – in PowerPoint 2002, Internet Explorer and on machines which have neither installed.

Covers

Chapter Five

The PowerPoint 2002 screen

Below is a detailed illustration of the PowerPoint 2002 screen:

Click this tab to view a text outline or this tab for icons representing slides. (Clicking a slide's entry here displays it in the Slide area.)

You can enter speaker notes into Notes view. Carry out the following procedure:

Click in Notes view. Type in the relevant text. When you've finished, click back in the Slide area.

Title bar   Menu bar   Rulers

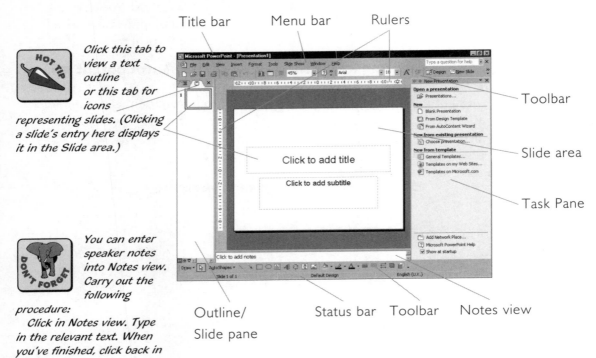

Toolbar

Slide area

Task Pane

Outline/ Slide pane   Status bar   Toolbar   Notes view

Some of these components can be hidden, if required.

Specifying which screen components display

Pull down the Tools menu and click Options. Then:

1 Ensure the View tab is active

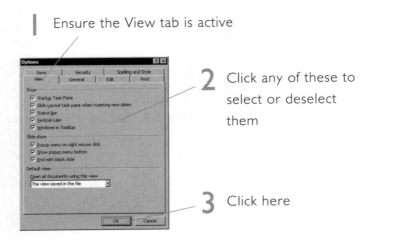

2 Click any of these to select or deselect them

3 Click here

The AutoContent Wizard

In chapter 1, we looked at how to create new Office documents based on templates and Wizards. PowerPoint 2002 has a unique and particularly detailed Wizard which handles the basics of creating a presentation.

Creating a new slide show via the AutoContent Wizard

1 In the Task Pane on the right of the screen, click General Templates

2 Ensure this tab is active

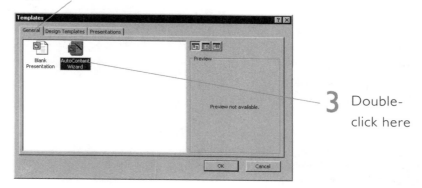

3 Double-click here

PowerPoint now launches the Wizard. Do the following:

The Wizard produces a 'standard' slide show which you can amend later, if you want.

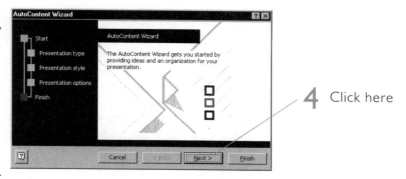

4 Click here

See Chapter 1 for how to create a blank presentation, or a slide show based on a template.

Complete the remaining four dialogs in the normal way. In the final AutoContent dialog, click Finish to have PowerPoint generate the presentation.

The slide views – an overview

PowerPoint has the following views:

Normal	displays each slide individually
Slide Sorter	shows all the slides as icons, so you can manipulate them more easily
Notes Page	shows each slide plus any speaker notes

Switching to a view

Pull down the View menu and click the relevant view entry.

The three views are compared below:

Normal view also includes the following additional views:

- *Outline/Slide view – shows the textual structure underlying slides (Outline) or thumbnails for each slide (Slide – a sort of mini Slide Sorter view)*

- *Notes view – shows the speaker notes associated with the active slide*

  See page 148 for a visual description.

These are different ways of looking at your slide show. Normal view provides a very useful overview, while Slide Sorter view lets you modify more than one slide at a time.

Normal view

Slide Sorter view

Notes Page view

Using the slide views

All the views have their own default magnification. You can adjust this, however.

Pull down the View menu and click Zoom. Do the following:

A Click a Zoom %

B Click here

You can also use Slide Sorter view to perform additional operations – for instance, you can use it to apply a new slide layout (see page 153) to more than one slide at a time.

The following are some brief supplementary notes on how best to use the PowerPoint 2002 views.

Normal view

Normal view displays the current slide in its own window. Use Normal view when you want a detailed picture of a slide (for instance, when you amend any of the slide contents, or when you change the overall formatting).

You can also use Normal view to:

- work with text. The Outline component of the Outline/ Slide pane (see the HOT TIP on page 148) displays only text. You can amend this and watch your changes take effect in the Slide area on the right

- enter notes. Simply click in the Notes view below the Slide area and enter speaker note text. (You can also do this within Notes Page view – see below)

To switch from slide to slide, you can press Page Up or Page Down as appropriate. (For more information on how to move around in presentations, see 'Moving through presentations' on page 160.)

Slide Sorter view

If you need to rearrange the order of slides, use Slide Sorter view. You can simply click on a slide and drag it to a new location (to move more than one slide, hold down one Ctrl key as you click them, then release the key and drag). You can also copy a slide by holding down Ctrl as you drag.

Notes Page view

This view is an aid to the presenter rather than the viewer of the slide show. If you want to enter speaker notes on a slide (for later printing), use Notes Page view.

In Notes Page view, the slide is displayed at a reduced size at the top of the page. Below this is a standard PowerPoint 2002 text object. For how to enter notes in this, see the 'Adding text to slides' topic on page 154.

Using grids

You can add a grid to slides within Normal or Notes Page views. This is a useful feature because you can align objects (e.g. pictures) to it.

Enabling the grid

In Normal or Notes Page view, pull down the View menu and select Grid and Guides

Ensure Snap objects to grid is ticked to have objects 'attracted' to the grid.

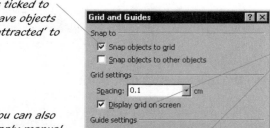

2 Ensure Display grid on screen is ticked then confirm

You can also apply manual ('drawing') guides. Ensure Display drawing guides on screen is ticked.

The grid structure

A drawing guide – you can drag this to a new location (as here) and align objects to it

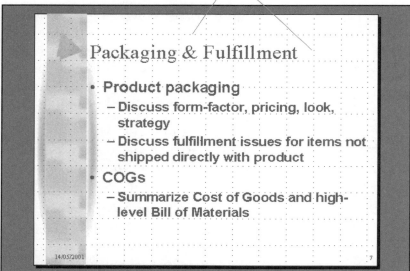

Customising slide structure

You can select more than one slide in Slide Sorter view by holding down Ctrl as you click on the slide icons.

The easiest way to customise the basic format of a slide is to use preset layouts. There are almost 30 of these under various headings (Text, Content, Text and Content and Other). You can apply layouts to one or more slides. When you've done this, you can then amend the individual components (see later topics).

Using preset layouts

You can also use the Slide component of the Outline/ Slide pane to select multiple slides:

Make sure you're in Slide or Slide Sorter view. If you're in Slide Sorter view, click the slide(s) you want to amend. Pull down the Format menu and click Slide Layout.

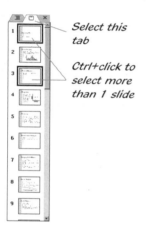

Select this tab

Ctrl+click to select more than 1 slide

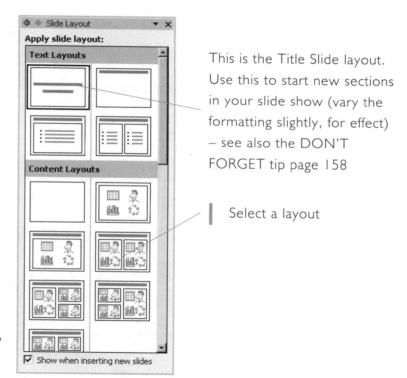

This is the Title Slide layout. Use this to start new sections in your slide show (vary the formatting slightly, for effect) – see also the DON'T FORGET tip page 158

Select a layout

Standard mouse techniques can be used to reposition or rescale text objects in PowerPoint 2002.

2 Any slide components present before you applied the new format will still remain. However, they may need to be resized or moved.

Adding text to slides

When you create a new slide show, PowerPoint 2002 fills each slide with placeholders containing sample text. The idea is that you should replace this with your own text.

The illustration below shows a sample slide before customisation:

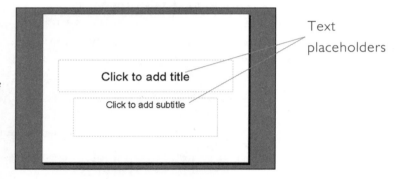

To insert your own text, click in any text placeholder. PowerPoint displays a text entry box. Now do the following:

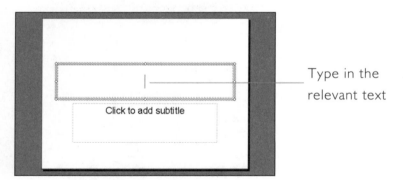

Finally, click anywhere outside the placeholder to confirm the addition of the new text.

Formatting text

You can format text in a variety of ways. You can:

- change the font and/or type size

- apply a font style or effect

- apply a colour

- specify the alignment

- specify the line spacing

Font-based formatting

Click inside the relevant text object and select the text you want to format. Pull down the Format menu and click Font. Now carry out any of steps 1-4 below, as appropriate. If you want to re-colour the text, carry out steps 5-6. Finally, follow step 7:

1 Click a new typeface

2 Type in a new point size

7 Click here

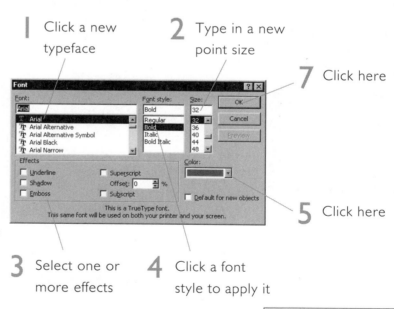

Re step 6 – if none of the colours here are suitable, click More Colors. In the Colors dialog, ensure the Standard tab is active. Click a colour in the polygon in the centre. Then click OK. Finally, follow step 7.

3 Select one or more effects

4 Click a font style to apply it

5 Click here

6 Click a colour (see the tip)

Changing text spacing

First, click inside the relevant text object and select the text whose spacing you want to amend. Pull down the Format menu and click Line Spacing. Now carry out any of steps 1-3 below, as appropriate. Then follow step 4.

You can summarise specific slides. When you do this, PowerPoint 2002 collects the slide titles and inserts them into a new slide.

In Slide Sorter view, select the relevant slides (they must contain titles). Then click the Summary Slide button:

in the Slide Sorter toolbar. The new slide is inserted in front of the first selected slide.

Type in a line spacing

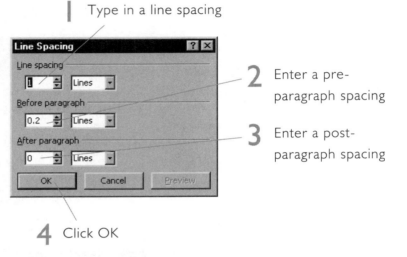

2 Enter a pre-paragraph spacing

3 Enter a post-paragraph spacing

4 Click OK

A summary slide

Changing text alignment

First, click inside the relevant text object and select the text whose alignment you want to amend. Pull down the Format menu and do the following:

Click here

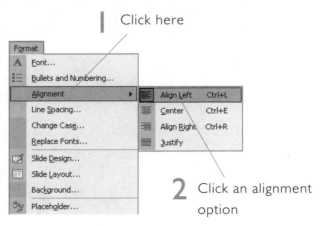

2 Click an alignment option

Colour schemes and design templates

Applying a new colour scheme or design template is a quick and effective way to give a presentation a new and consistent look.

Any PowerPoint presentation (apart from a blank one) has various colour schemes/design templates available to it.

Imposing a colour scheme/design template

| Pull down the Format menu and click Slide Design

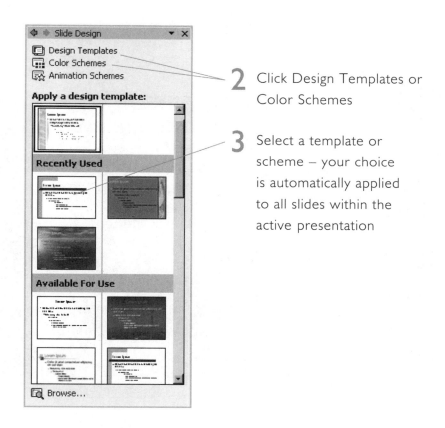

2 Click Design Templates or Color Schemes

3 Select a template or scheme – your choice is automatically applied to all slides within the active presentation

Slide masters

Re step 2 under 'Editing slide masters' — you can change the text formatting but not the text itself (you do this in the normal way on individual slides). To do this, click in a text placeholder and make any formatting changes.

When you apply a design template, PowerPoint automatically adds a 'slide master' to your presentation. The idea of slide masters is that you can change or add an element and have this automatically reflected in all the associated slides. Typical uses for slide masters include:

* inserting pictures (e.g. logos) which you want to appear on all slides

* implementing font formatting which you want to appear on all slides

Editing slide masters

Pull down the View menu and click Master, Slide Master

PowerPoint 2002 slide shows can have multiple slide masters.

Most slide masters are associated with title masters — use these to adjust slides which use a title slide layout. (See page 153 for how to use slide layouts.)

Here, 2 slide masters are shown — each has a title master

2 Edit the master (e.g. by reformatting text or adding pictures)

Format Painter

You can also use Format Painter to copy formatting between objects (e.g. pictures/clip art).

PowerPoint 2002 offers a useful shortcut (the Format Painter) which enables you to copy a colour scheme:

- from one presentation to a single slide in another
- from one presentation to multiple slides in another

Copying colour schemes

1 With both presentations open in Normal view, pull down the Window menu and click Arrange All

If the Standard toolbar isn't currently on-screen, pull down the View menu and click Toolbars, Standard.

2 Carry out step 3 below. In step 4, single-click for one copy or double-click for multiple copies (and see the HOT TIP):

4 Click or double-click the Format Painter icon in the Standard toolbar:

3 Click the icon representing the slide whose scheme you want to copy

To copy the formatting to more than one slide, double-click in step 4. In step 5, click as many icons as required. When you've finished, press Esc.

To use Format Painter to copy colour schemes, ensure the Slide tab of the Outline/Slide pane is enabled.

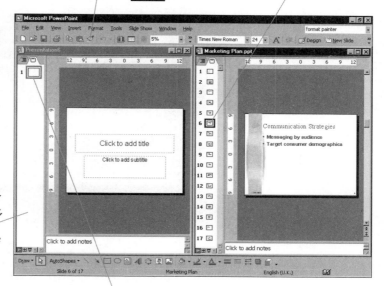

5 Click the icon representing the slide you want to format

Moving through presentations

Since presentations – by their very nature – always have more than one slide, it's essential to be able to move from slide to slide easily (it's even more essential in the case of especially large presentations). There are two main methods you can use to do this.

Using the vertical scroll bar

PowerPoint lets you broadcast slide shows over Intranets. For help with any aspect of slide show broadcasting (inc. scheduling the broadcast via Outlook), see your system administrator.

In Normal or Notes Page views, move the mouse pointer over the vertical scroll box. Hold down the left mouse button and drag the box up or down. As you do so, PowerPoint 2002 displays a message box giving you the number and title of the slide you're up to.

Slide number indicator – when the correct number displays, release the mouse button to jump to that slide

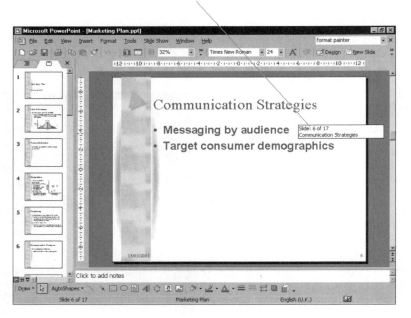

Using Slide Sorter view

Slide Sorter view offers a useful shortcut which you can use to jump immediately to a specific slide. Simply double-click any slide icon within Slide Sorter view; PowerPoint then switches to Slide view and displays the slide you selected.

Inserting and deleting slides

You can easily include existing slides from another slide show.

In Normal view, go to the slide after which you want the new slides inserted. Pull down the Insert menu and click Slides from Files. In the File field in the Slide Finder dialog, type in the address and file name of the second slide show. Click Display. In the Select slides section, click the slide(s) you want to include. Finally, click Insert.

You'll often want to insert a new slide into presentations. There are also occasions when you'll need to delete a slide because it's no longer required. PowerPoint 2002 lets you do both easily and conveniently.

Inserting a slide

1 In Normal or Notes Page views, move to the slide that you want to precede the new one. In Slide Sorter view, click the relevant slide

2 Pull down the Insert menu and click New Slide

To delete a slide in Normal or Notes Page views, move to the slide that you want to delete. In Slide Sorter view, click a slide (or hold down Ctrl as you click multiple slide icons to delete more than one slide). Then pull down the Edit menu and click Delete Slide.

(When you delete a slide, the slide and its contents are erased immediately, with no preliminary warning, although you can undo the deletion by pressing Ctrl+Z.)

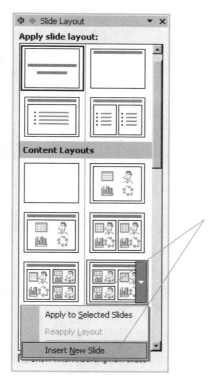

3 Right-click a layout – in the menu, click Insert New Slide

Inserting pictures

Once inserted into a worksheet, pictures can be resized and moved in the normal way.

Inserting pictures via the Insert Clip Art Task Pane

In Normal or Notes Page views, go to the slide into which you want the clip art added. Pull down the Insert menu and click Picture, Clip Art. Now carry out the following steps:

Enter one or more keywords

Clips have associated keywords. You can use these to locate clips.

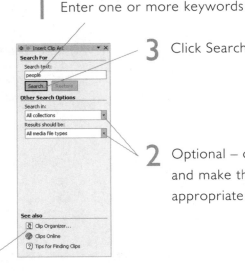

3 Click Search

2 Optional – click here and make the appropriate choices

You can add new clips to collections (or add new keywords to existing clips) in the Clip Organizer.
Click here to launch it:

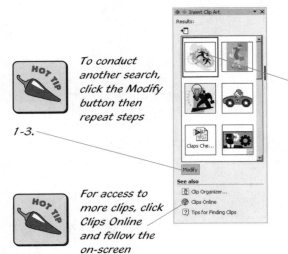

To conduct another search, click the Modify button then repeat steps 1-3.

4 Click an icon to insert the clip

For access to more clips, click Clips Online and follow the on-screen instructions.

To have a picture appear on every slide, insert it into the slide master (a template which applies to the overall slide show).

Pull down the View menu and click Master, Slide Master. Now insert a picture. To return to the active slide, do the following:

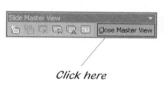

Click here

See page 158 for more on slide masters.

PowerPoint 2002 provides a preview of what the picture will look like when it's been imported – see the Preview box on the right of the dialog.

If this isn't visible, click the following toolbar icon repeatedly until it is:

Inserting pictures – the dialog route

In Normal or Notes Page views, go to the slide into which you want the picture added. Pull down the Insert menu and do the following:

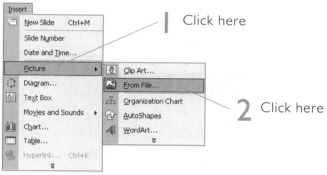

| Click here

2 Click here

4 Click here. In the drop-down list, click the drive/folder that hosts the picture

6 Click here

3 Make sure All Pictures... is showing. If it isn't, click the arrow and select it from the drop-down list

5 Click a picture file

Inserting diagrams

You can insert diagrams (e.g. pyramids and org charts) into slides.

| In Normal or Notes Page view, pull down the Insert menu and click Diagram

2 Click a diagram

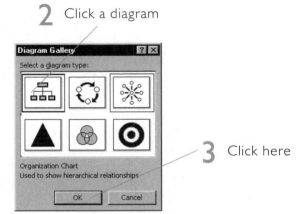

3 Click here

Clicking a text placeholder launches the Diagram toolbar. Use this to make any further changes e.g.:

Click here to transform the diagram into another

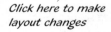

Click here to make layout changes

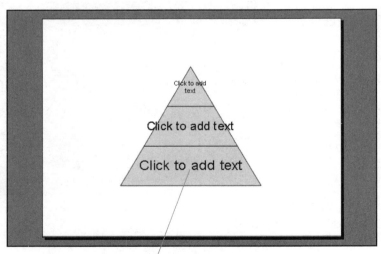

An inserted pyramid – edit it as required e.g. click a text placeholder and type in text

Inserting animations

To add a custom animation, go to the relevant slide in Normal view. Click the object you want to animate. Pull down the Slide Show menu and click Custom Animation. In the Custom Animation Task Pane, click the Add Effect button. In the menu, select a category; in the submenu, select an effect.
   Do the following:

You can apply animations to slides. In PowerPoint, animations are defined as visual/sound effects applied to text and/or objects. You can apply standard animation schemes (often the best idea) or you can apply customised effects to specific objects.

Applying an animation scheme

1 Optional – in Slide Sorter view, select the slides you want to animate

2 Pull down the Slide Show menu and click Animation Schemes

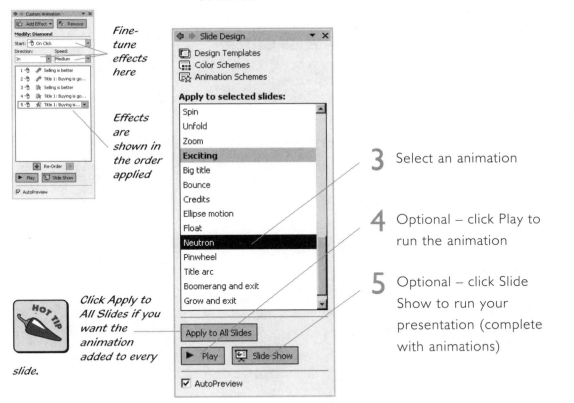

Fine-tune effects here

Effects are shown in the order applied

3 Select an animation

4 Optional – click Play to run the animation

5 Optional – click Slide Show to run your presentation (complete with animations)

Click Apply to All Slides if you want the animation added to every slide.

Inserting hyperlinks

You can insert hyperlinks into slides. In PowerPoint 2002, hyperlinks are 'action buttons' which you can click (while a presentation is being run) to jump to a prearranged destination immediately. This can be:

- preset slide targets (for instance, the first, last, next or previous slide)

- a specific slide (where *you* select a slide from a special dialog)

- a URL (providing you have a live Internet connection)

- another PowerPoint presentation

- another file

'URL' stands for Uniform Resource Locator. URLs are unique addresses for World Wide Web sites.

Inserting an action button

In Normal or Notes Page view, pull down the Slide Show menu. Do the following:

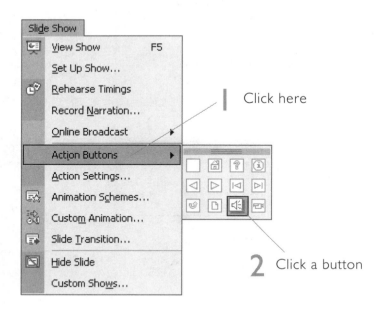

Click here

2 Click a button

3 Position the mouse pointer at the location on the slide where you want the button inserted. Drag to define the button

4 Click here

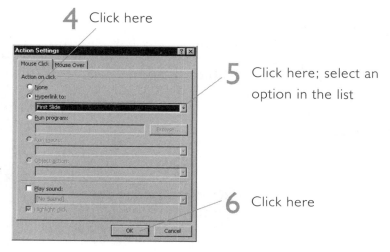

5 Click here; select an option in the list

Re. step 4 – complete any further dialog which launches. Click OK, then follow step 5.

6 Click here

The illustration below shows an inserted action button/ hyperlink:

Hyperlinks only become active when you run your slide show.

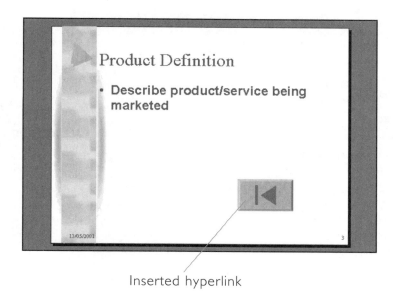

Inserted hyperlink

Printing

To preview a slide before printing, press Ctrl+F2. The Print Preview window launches:

Press Esc to close it.

You can print any presentation component. These include:

- slides

- speaker notes

- outlines

PowerPoint 2002 makes printing easy.

Printing a presentation

Pull down the File menu and click Print. Now carry out any of steps 1-5 below, as appropriate. Finally, follow step 6.

Ensure 'Grayscale' and 'Pure Black and White' are deselected here if you have a colour printer and want to print out in colour.

Re step 4 – separate non-adjacent slides with commas but no spaces – e.g. to print slides 2, 5, 7 and 9 type in:

2,5,7,9

Enter contiguous slides with dashes – e.g. to print slides 2 to 7 inclusive, type in:

2-7

1 Click here; select the printer you want from the list

2 Click here to print the current slide only

3 Type in the number of copies required

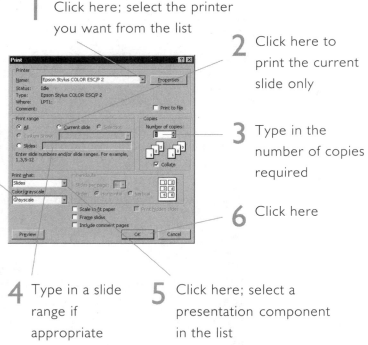

6 Click here

4 Type in a slide range if appropriate

5 Click here; select a presentation component in the list

Fast-track printing

To print using all the current settings, without launching the Print dialog, simply click this button on the Standard toolbar:

Running a presentation

Once you've created (and possibly printed) your slide show, it's time to run it. Before you do so, however, you should set the run parameters.

If you export slide shows to HTML format (see pages 171-172), you can view and run them in Internet Explorer.

When you run your presentation you can, if you want, have PowerPoint 2002 wait for your command before moving from slide to slide. This is useful if you anticipate being interrupted during the presentation. You retain full control over delivery.

Alternatively, you can have the slide show run automatically. Before you can do this, though, you have to set various parameters. These include the intervals between slides, which slides you want to run and the presentation type.

Preparing to run your slide show

First, open the presentation you want to run. Then pull down the Slide Show menu and click Set Up Show. Now do the following:

You can choose from a wide variety of slide show types. The first option (presentation by a speaker) is the most common.

| If you don't want all the slides to run, enter start and end slide numbers

Re step 2 – click 'Using timings, if present' option to have the presentation run automatically.

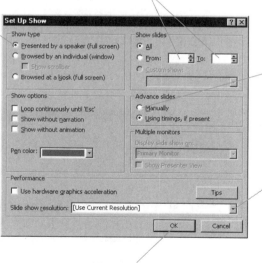

2 Select Manually if you want to control the slide progression manually

3 Optional – click here; select a resolution in the list

4 Click here

Running a manual presentation

Pull down the Slide Show menu and click View Show. If you selected Manually in step 2 on page 169, PowerPoint 2002 runs the first slide of your presentation and pauses. When you're ready to move on to the next slide, left-click once or press Page Down. If you need to go back to the previous slide, simply press Page Up as often as required.

Rehearsing an automatic presentation

Before you can run an automatic presentation, you have to set the slide intervals. You can do this by 'rehearsing' the slide show. Pull down the Slide Show menu and click Rehearse Timings, then do the following:

If you want to end your slide show at any time, simply press Esc. This applies to manual and automatic presentations.

This timer counts the interval until the next slide; when the timing is right, follow step 1

For an automatic slide show, follow step 1 as often as necessary before you run it.

| Click here

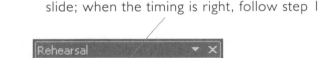

After step 1, PowerPoint moves to the next slide. Repeat step 1 until all the slides have had appropriate intervals allocated. Finally, do the following:

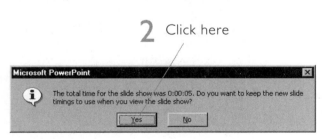

2 Click here

You can also run your slide show on another computer (even one on which PowerPoint and Internet Explorer haven't been installed).
  Pull down the File menu and click Pack and Go – this launches the Pack and Go Wizard. Follow the on-screen instructions.

Running an automatic presentation

After rehearsal, pull down the Slide Show menu and click View Show. If you clicked 'Using timings, if present' in step 2 on page 169, PowerPoint 2002 displays the first slide and moves on to subsequent slides after the rehearsed intervals have elapsed.

Running presentations in Explorer

B. means that slide shows converted to HTML format and saved to the Web can be run by the majority of Internet users.

One corollary of Microsoft's elevation of the HTML format to a status which rivals that of its own formats is that:

A.   presentations display authentically in Internet Explorer (especially if you're using version 4 or above)

B.   you can even run presentations from within Internet Explorer

Running slide shows in Internet Explorer

First, use the techniques discussed on page 17 ('Saving to shortcuts') to convert an existing presentation to HTML format. Open this in Internet Explorer. Now do the following:

Click here to run your show in Full-Screen mode

You can hide the slide outline, if you want. Simply click here:
(Repeat to unhide it.)

Here, the slide show is being displayed in Internet Explorer 5.5.

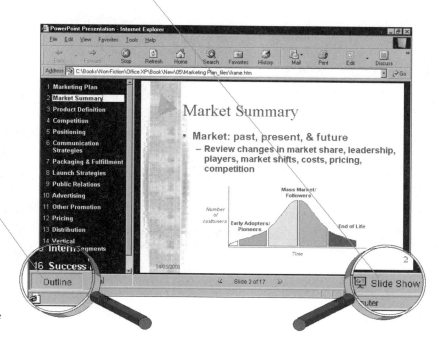

Internet Explorer now launches the first slide of your presentation so that it occupies the whole screen:

For further coverage of essential PowerPoint 2002 features, see 'PowerPoint 2002', also in the 'in easy steps' series.

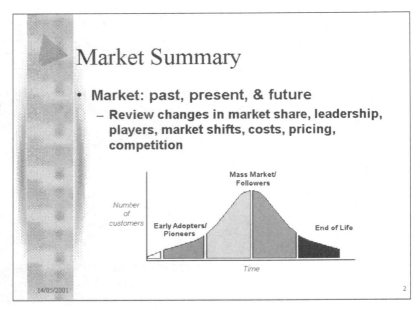

To halt the slide show before the end, press Esc.

Whether or not you selected 'Using timings, if present' in step 2 on page 169, Internet Explorer progresses to the next slide when the relevant interval has elapsed. And so on to the end...

When the last slide has been displayed, a special screen displays with the following text:

To close Internet Explorer, press Alt+F4.

End of slide show, click to exit.

Click anywhere to return to Internet Explorer's main screen.

Outlook 2002

This chapter explores the stand-alone (i.e. non-workgroup) use of Outlook 2002. You'll use the Outlook bar to launch any of Outlook's associated folders, then enter colour-coded appointments, events, tasks and contact details; Outlook 2002 will then coordinate them so that you can manage your business/personal affairs more easily. You'll also use Outlook 2002 to compose, transmit, receive and reply to e-mail, using (optimally) Word 2002 as your editor and working with multiple accounts. Finally, you'll housekeep your Mailbox, and surf the Internet directly from within Outlook 2002.

Covers

Chapter Six

The Outlook 2002 screen

The Folder banner tells you which Outlook folder (in this case, Inbox) is active.

To print out work you do in any component on the Outlook bar, first click the relevant folder. Press Ctrl+P. Complete the Print dialog as normal. In particular, select a print style – the choices vary with the folder selected. Finally, click OK to begin printing.

Below is a detailed illustration of a typical Outlook 2002 screen.

Title bar   Menu bar   Toolbar

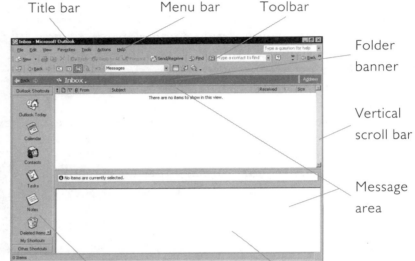

Folder banner

Vertical scroll bar

Message area

Outlook bar displaying folders   Preview pane

Some of these – e.g. the Menu and scroll bars – are standard to just about all Windows programs. However, you can specify which of the four available toolbars display.

Specifying which toolbars display
Pull down the View menu and do the following:

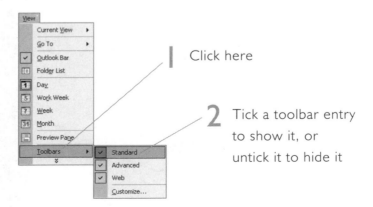

Click here

2 Tick a toolbar entry to show it, or untick it to hide it

Using the Outlook bar

Outlook 2002 organises its features into folders. All folders are accessible from the Outlook bar.

When you run Outlook 2002, it automatically opens the Inbox, the folder in which incoming messages are stored. This provides access to often used features. However, there are several additional folders you can access. These include:

Outlook Today	Provides a handy summary of mail, tasks and appointments
Calendar	A tool to help you schedule events, tasks, appointments and meetings
Contacts	A tool to help you manage business/personal contacts
Tasks	A task management aid
Notes	Acts as a pad; you can create 'sticky' notes
Outbox	Messages waiting to be sent are stored here
Deleted Items	Self-explanatory

To insert a note, click the Notes folder in the Outlook bar. Press Ctrl+N. Do the following:

Type in your note, then press Alt+F4.

Activating folders
Do the following:

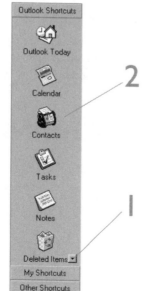

To access additional delivery-based features, click here:

My Shortcuts

To access Windows folders, click here:

Other Shortcuts

2 Click a folder icon

| Optional – click the arrow to view more folder icons

The Calendar – an overview

The Calendar provides alternative ways of viewing and interacting with your schedules. The main views are:

Day/Week/Month

The all-purpose view. An aspect of the Appointment Book; used to enter appointments, events and tasks. You can specify whether you work in the Day, Work Week, Week or Month aspects. (See below)

Active Appointments

An aspect of the Appointment Book; used to enter and monitor active appointments

Events

An aspect of the Appointment Book, useful for entering and monitoring events

Some aspects of Outlook 2002 – for instance, the use of the Calendar to coordinate meetings among workgroup members – are beyond the scope of this book.

Switching between the Day, Work Week, Week and Month Calendars

You'll probably use Day/Week/Month view more than any other, because it offers great flexibility. By default, this view displays appointments etc. with the use of the Day aspect. To change the aspect, refer to the Standard toolbar and do the following:

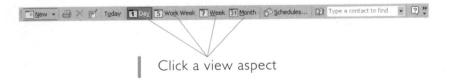

Click a view aspect

Using the Day Calendar

Re step 2 – if the date shown in the Date Navigator isn't correct, click:

 or ▶

to go back or forward by one month respectively.

If you need to mark a meeting as recurring, carry out steps 1-3. Then double-click the appointment. In the toolbar within the dialog which launches, click this button:

In the Appointment Recurrence dialog, set the relevant options. Click OK. Now click the following:

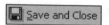

To edit an appointment, double-click it in the Calendar. Complete the dialog – for example, click in the Label field and do the following:

Colour-code the appointment

You can add appointments to the Day Calendar.

If you want, you can stipulate that the appointment is recurring (i.e. it's automatically entered at an interval you specify).

Adding an appointment in the Day Calendar

Carry out steps 1, 2 and 3 below (then follow the procedures in the DON'T FORGET tip if you want to mark the appointment as recurring):

An inserted event – see overleaf

2 Click the correct day

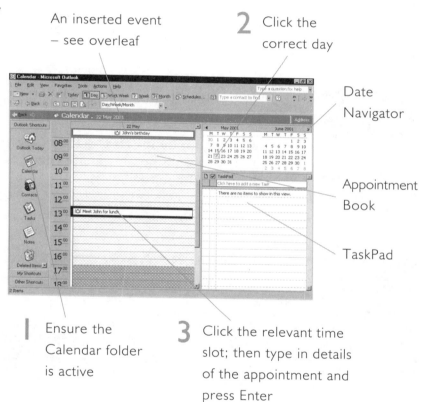

Date Navigator

Appointment Book

TaskPad

| Ensure the Calendar folder is active

3 Click the relevant time slot; then type in details of the appointment and press Enter

Outlook adds the new appointment to the Calendar.

You can add events to the Daily Calendar.

Outlook 2002 handles events in a rather different way to appointments. For example, they don't occupy specific time slots in your Appointment Book. Instead, they can relate to any day and can even extend over more than one.

If you need to amend or update an existing event, double-click its button within the Appointment Book:

Outlook 2002 distinguishes between events and annual events. Annual events occur yearly on a specific date.

Examples of events include:

John's birthday

Now follow steps 1-3 here, as appropriate.

- birthdays and anniversaries

- shows

- seminars

Re step 1 – to mark an event as annual, click Recurrence. In the dialog, select Yearly (and complete any further fields). Click OK.

Events display as buttons within the Appointment Book (see page 177).

Adding an event to the Day Calendar

Pull down the Actions menu and click New All Day Event. Now do the following:

3 Click here   2 Enter a description

To mark an event as recurring, click the Recurrence button after steps 1-2. In the dialog which launches, set the relevant options. Click OK. Now perform step 3.

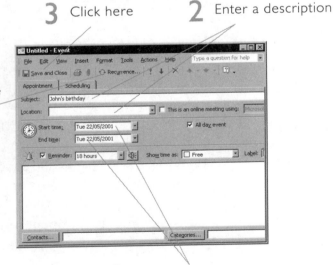

Type in start and end dates

Using the Week Calendars

You have to use a slightly different procedure to add appointments.
Press Ctrl+N. Carry out steps 2-4 on page 180.

Use the Work Week or Week views as an alternative way to display your appointments and events.

In the Week Calendars, you can enter events and appointments. Enter events using the same procedures as for Day view. For appointments, see the HOT TIP.

Moving around in the Week Calendars

Pull down the View menu and click Go To, Go to Date. Carry out steps 1-4 and 7 to jump to a specific date in the Week Calendars, OR steps 5-7 as an alternative way to switch between views:

I Click here

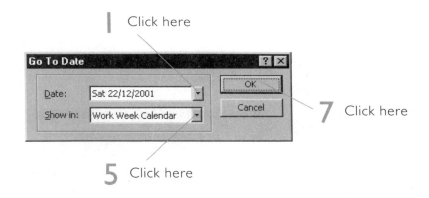

7 Click here

5 Click here

For further coverage of essential Outlook 2002 features, see 'Outlook 2002', also in the 'in easy steps' series.

2 Optional – click here to move I month back

3 Optional – click here to move I month forward

4 Click the day you want to view

6 Select a Calendar view

Day Calendar
Week Calendar
Month Calendar
Work Week Calendar

Using the Month Calendar

You can use the Find tool in folders to locate specific data.
If the Find tool isn't already displaying at the top of the screen, press Ctrl+E. Do the following:

Use the Month Calendar to gain a useful overview of your schedule.

Inserting a new appointment in the Month Calendar

Pull down the Actions menu and do the following:

A Enter search data

B Click Find Now

Any matches are shown below the Find window.

Click here

4 Click here   **3** Enter a description

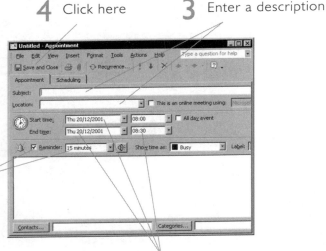

Click Reminder (then insert a reminder interval in the field to the right) if you want Outlook 2002 to prompt you when an appointment is due.

2 Type in start and end dates and times

Inserting a new event in the Monthly Calendar

You can insert events in the Monthly Calendar by using the same techniques as for the Daily Calendar. Carry out steps 1-3 on page 178.

Working with the Tasks folder

Use the Tasks folder to enter and track tasks.

When you've entered a task into the Tasks folder, it displays in the TaskPad in the Daily, Work Week and Week Calendars and in Outlook Today.

If you need to amend or update an existing task, click within it and follow steps 1 and 2.

Entering a task

If the Tasks folder isn't already active, click the Tasks icon in the Outlook bar. Then do the following:

Various views are available in the Tasks folder (the view shown here is 'Simple List').

To switch between views, click Current View in the View menu; select a view in the sub-menu.

2 Type in a due date, then press Enter

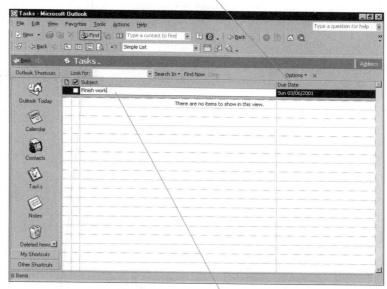

Click here; type in a task description

Tasks can be prioritised (Outlook recognises three levels: Low, Normal and High – Normal is the default).

To set a priority, click the Priority field and select one in the list.

Customising tasks

The above steps produce a basic task. If you want to customise the settings in more depth (for instance, you can set start and end dates, reminder intervals and/or priority levels – see the DON'T FORGET tip), double-click the task after step 2. Complete the dialog which launches, then click Save and Close.

Working with the Contacts folder

Another view – Detailed Address Cards – uses the card model but with even more detail...

Use the Contacts folder as a convenient place to keep track of business/personal contacts.

Outlook displays contacts in various forms. The two main aspects are:

*   as a grid

*   using a business card model

To switch between views, click Current View in the View menu; select a view in the sub-menu.

You can enter contacts directly into either, but you may find that the business card view makes the job easier.

Entering a contact

If the Contacts view isn't already active, click the Contacts icon in the Outlook bar. Then do the following:

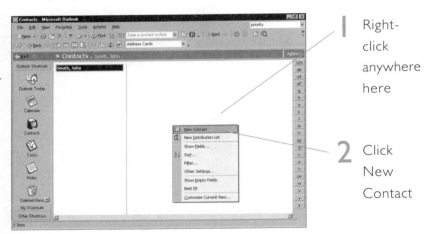

If you need to amend a contact, double-click it. Then carry out steps 3-4 as appropriate.

To use Outlook as your default email client, follow the procedures in page 44's DON'T FORGET tip.

1 Right-click anywhere here

2 Click New Contact

To set advanced contact details, click the additional dialog tabs. Complete the relevant fields then carry out step 4.

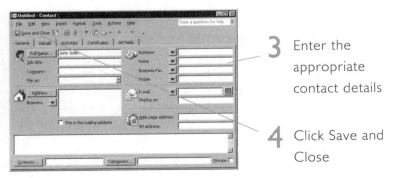

3 Enter the appropriate contact details

4 Click Save and Close

Composing e-mail

When you first launch it, Outlook runs the Outlook 2002 Startup wizard. Among other things, this specifies which e-mail service options you use. There are two main choices. You can opt to connect via a phone line or by a local area network (LAN).

The Startup wizard customises Outlook 2002 in line with the above (and further) choices made. As a result, you should have no difficulty in carrying out the instructions given here and later.

Composing e-mail

If the Inbox isn't currently open, click the Inbox icon in the Outlook bar. Pull down the File menu and click New, Mail Message. Do the following:

4 Click Send

1 Type in the email address (Outlook recognises and completes addresses from email you've already sent)

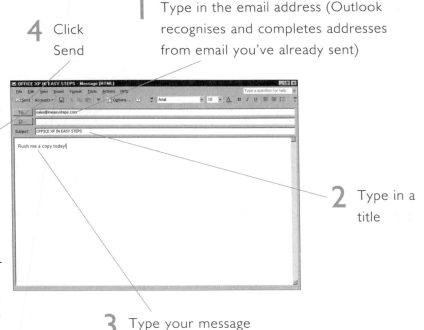

2 Type in a title

3 Type your message

Reading and replying to e-mail

When you reply to e-mail, Outlook uses the format in which the original mail was sent.

Reading e-mail

Once e-mail has been downloaded to you, you can read it in two ways. Do ONE of the following:

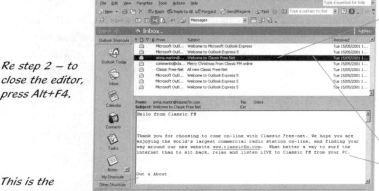

Re step 2 – to close the editor, press Alt+F4.

2 Double-click a message here; read the mail in the editor which launches

Click an email & read it here

This is the Preview pane: use it as a shortcut for viewing mail.

Replying to e-mail

Carry out the following steps:

1 Click this button: in the original message's overhead bar

Here, Outlook 2002 has launched its own email editor.

(If you've followed the Tool Options dialog procedure in the HOT TIP on page 183, Word 2002 will launch instead.)

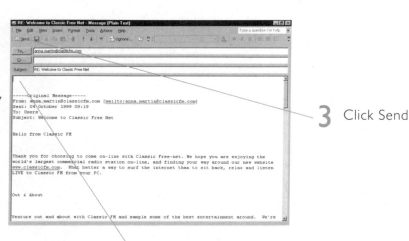

3 Click Send

2 Type in your reply at the head of the message

Sending/receiving e-mail

If you use more than one email service (this includes Hotmail), you can set up multiple email accounts.

Pull down the Tools menu and choose E-Mail Accounts. In the E-mail Accounts dialog, select Add a new e-mail account and click Next. Complete the remaining dialogs.

You can carry out housekeeping tasks on your Mailbox – for instance, you can have Outlook 'archive' old mail items (i.e. move them to the Archive Folders folder) or you can have it empty the Deleted Items folder...

Pull down the Tools menu and select Mailbox Cleanup. Complete the Mailbox Cleanup dialog and click OK.

After sending and (if applicable) downloading mail, by default Outlook 2002 closes your Internet connection.

To send (and simultaneously receive) e-mail via an Internet Service Provider, do the following from within any of the e-mail related folders:

1 Click Send/Receive

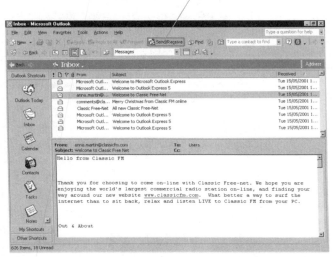

2 Outlook 2002 establishes a connection to your Internet Service Provider and sends your e-mail. After this, it downloads any mail waiting for you

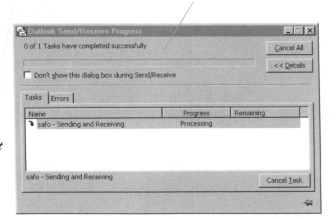

Surfing the Internet

You can:

- view Web pages directly from within Outlook 2002

- send Web pages as part of e-mail messages

Viewing Web pages

First, make sure your Internet connection is live. Refer to the Web toolbar (if isn't visible, click Toolbars, Web in the View menu) and do the following:

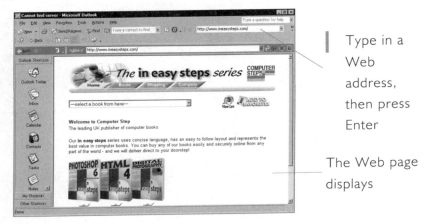

Type in a Web address, then press Enter

The Web page displays

Sending Web pages

After you've carried out step 1 above (though not necessarily while you're still online), pull down the Actions menu and do the following:

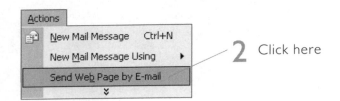

2 Click here

Outlook launches a new e-mail message with the Web page pre-loaded. Perform steps 1-4 on page 183. Then, if you went offline to carry out step 2 above, carry out the procedures on page 185 to send your Web page/message.

Index

A

B

C

D

E

F

P